THE CHURCH IN A NEW IRELAND

COLUMBA EXPLORATIONS 2

The Church in a new Ireland

Edited by

Seán MacRéamoinn

the columba press

First published in 1996 by
the columba press
55A Spruce Avenue, Stillorgan Industrial Park,
Blackrock, Co Dublin

Cover by Bill Bolger
Origination by The Columba Press
Printed in Ireland by Genprint Ltd., Dublin

ISBN 1 85607 170 7

Contents

Foreword

To live is to change, to grow is to change often ... Following Newman's maxim, these years of great and rapid change in our society should also be years of great and rapid growth for the church. The present reality in Ireland is quite different, and the implications of the situation provide the subject of this second volume of *Columba Explorations*.

This is clearly a matter of concern for all Christians, north and south. However, our four main essays (as well as the editor's introduction) come from the experience of the majority church in the Republic. These are followed by a response deriving from northern Presbyterian experience and outlook.

As in our first *Exploration*, we offer all six essays as a contribution to a critical awareness of where we stand, and to the promotion of a spirit of creative renewal.

Introduction:
Living with Change

Seán MacRéamoinn

'*What is the church for?* This is the question ...' says our essayist Sister Carol Dorgan, and in asking it she touches the
heart of the matter of this book. It's not the sort of question
you'd hear a generation or two ago because, I suppose, the
answer was seen to be self-evident. We all knew what the
church was for, even if we mightn't be good at putting it
into words.

For, from time immemorial, as they used to say, the vast
majority of Irish children were baptised into the church of
Christ, and we all grew up in it, like our fathers and mothers
before us. Like them too, most of us were Catholics,
though some were Protestants (a few were neither, being
of the Jewish faith – or even, a very few, of no religion). So
the church and the churches were part of our daily lives, of
our landscape – literally, in the bricks and mortar sense,
but also the landscape of our thinking and imagining.

But not any more, not universally so, nor anything like it.
Certainly most of our children are still baptised, and we
can claim an impressive church-going majority; but not as
impressive as it was forty, thirty or even fifteen years ago.
As our first contributor, Anne Looney, says, 'We are a
changed people living in a changed place.' And, she adds,
'it is the pace of change that disturbs people as much as the
results of change.'

The two sections of our people where the change is most

visible and most radical are the poor, notably the urban poor – as Carol Dorgan makes vividly clear – and the young, children of the ongoing cultural revolution which began here in the sixties. But change is not neatly to be contained in this or that social box; it spills out all over, flooding familiar fields and uprooting longstanding landmarks.

It is, as Anne Looney remarks, now possible to 'live a life in Ireland ... untouched by institutional religion. It's not so much a matter of ideological as a sort of *cultural* atheism.' And she goes on to say:

> Ask some of the adults who no longer practise their religion about the reasons why. The vast majority are puzzled by the question. They just ... *stopped*. Irish Catholicism is now seen as something you grow out of ...

So it is neither exaggeration nor alarmist rhetoric to say that the Irish, in these last years of the second millennium, are witnesses to the long-delayed but now rapid decline of a unique religious culture. Unique in its blend of Christian and pre-Christian elements – though with the former unmistakably dominant; unique too in its tenacity and vitality, despite persecution from without and, from within, a slow impoverishment mainly caused by the obscurantist philistinism of both religious and secular authority.

I say the decline, perhaps the demise, of a *culture*, not of a faith. For faith is a strange and subtle thing, God-given and God-sustained, often in spite of our worst efforts. Then there's *religion*, the system within which faith is seen to 'operate': and since it is a human construct it is subject to change and decay.

But for Christians, religion and the faith which informs it, live in the people, God's people whom we call the church. And here we have life on two levels: the divine life of the Spirit, which is immortal, and God's word made flesh, flesh living but mortal and corruptible. So indeed the church too may decline, though we have the Paschal promise that if it falls it will rise again. History records many times and places of decline, brought about by human action or circumstance. And if the church in Ireland is in decline just now – and many of us believe that it is – this is mainly due to the decline of the culture which sustained it for so long, which it took for granted, and on which it overmuch relied.

Looking Back
It is perhaps difficult for us now to realise how strong and pervasive that culture once was. Already deeply rooted in medieval Ireland, it survived the turmoil of the Reformation and subsequent religious conflict and, in modern times, the 'Protestant nation' of the eighteenth century finally yielded to 'Catholic Ireland' in the years after Emancipation. Ironically, it was then, in a process that came to full development in the century between 1850 and 1950, that much of immemorial tradition was lost and replaced by a mixture of ultramontanism, Italo-English devotionalism and a rigorism which would prescribe for every detail of Christian living.

So confident had the 'Catholic nation' become, that it was widely expected that Home Rule would indeed be closer to Rome Rule than reassuring protestations allowed. And though the Gaelic League, Sinn Féin, Connolly's socialism and Larkin's militant trades-unionism, together with a number of doctrinaire republicans and Anglo-Irish intellectuals, brought a new dimension to political culture, 'Catholic nationalism', as articulated by D. P. Moran of the *Leader* and others, was still alive and working.

In the event, the establishment of an Irish state which followed developments from 1913 to 1922, did not adopt a confessional Catholic constitution. But Catholic social thinking remained dominant and reached its apotheosis in the 'new' constitution of 1937, although its architect, Éamon de Valera – perhaps with a hopeful eye to reconciling the Protestant North – also kept clear of the confessional brink. Indeed de Valera showed his independence on more than one occasion, notably in his coolness to the Franco rebellion in Spain.

However, the crisis for Catholic church influence on public policy came in the early 1950s when, following the Noel Browne affair, popular opinion became more critical of what came to be seen as the improper interference of church authority. The fact that the government of the day had apparently canvassed and willingly accepted this 'interference' served to underline the impropriety. From then on, things began to change. Today bishops are rarely consulted by government except where institutional church interests are directly involved – and then often merely 'for information'.

So much for politics, which are not our present concern, except in so far as they have articulated a popular cultural consensus. And it is, I think, fair to say that for many years that was the case. Thus, the censorship of books and films did almost certainly reflect majority attitudes as, on a more serious level, did the lack of provision for divorce and remarriage. My point is that what might now be regarded as repressive legislation was for a long time in accord with the public will.

That will had been shaped and coloured not just by a church-related educational system, but by family tradition and community custom, as well as by popular history, literature and folkways. As to the mass media, the national press (with the exception of the then minority *Irish Times*) and radio were broadly supportive. The British press did not command a significant readership – except perhaps for some of the more colourful Sunday papers which were careful to publish an Irish edition, suitably sanitised. The BBC and, at one time, continental-based commercial radio, had their audiences, but had little serious influence (except perhaps during the Second World War when BBC news filled the gaps!)

There were, of course, comings and goings between Ireland and Britain, and to a much lesser extent America, and Australia. Journeys to continental Europe and further afield to Africa and Asia were, until well into the 1950s, mainly of religious motivation, so that returning travellers – pilgrims, missionaries, students – served to enhance the received worldview.

The only international gathering hosted by the Irish state before the war was also of a religious nature. This was the Eucharistic Congress of 1932 which brought several thousand pilgrims to Dublin, led by a Papal Cardinal Legate. It was an event of no small importance for Irish Catholic prestige, as well as a quite remarkable feat of organisation: nearly a million of the faithful attended the final Mass in Phoenix Park. Towns and villages were *en fête* and the papal colours and blue Congress flag were everywhere. G. K. Chesterton wrote:

> I did not merely take a ticket for Holyhead or a boat for the port of Dublin ... I did truly take a ticket for Christendom. I took a train and a boat that brought me to the ancient and perhaps long-undiscovered island that was once called Christendom. For it did truly appear as in a dream that the island had grown

large, and that I had landed in something larger than
a continent ...

Perhaps it was a similar dream that, nearly thirty years
later, inspired a smaller but no less proud gathering in
June 1961, a highpoint of the Patrician Year of 1961-2.
Again a Papal Legate was there, in Dublin's Theatre Royal,
to hear the then Taoiseach, Seán Lemass, declare: 'Whatever the future, this is the faith by which we shall live, this
is the rock on which we will continue to stand ...' The following St Patrick's Day, the Year ended in Rome when
President de Valera paid a state visit to Pope John XXIII.

A few months later, Pope John would inaugurate the
Second Vatican Council. Nothing would ever be the same
again. Still, looking back on those years, the last before the
great changes, I think not so much of the grand occasions
as of the small facts of Catholic life in the Ireland I grew up
in.

Mass-going, for example: an obligation – it was important
to 'get' Mass, but also a social occasion, especially in the
country; there was fasting if you were going to Holy
Communion, and this implied an early Mass. In towns
and cities there were those who were noted as always getting to the latest possible Mass, at the last minute ... but
nearly all of them got there, sometime. And a remarkable
number went on week-mornings, young and old alike –
especially in Lent. Unlike the class in Anne Looney's story
we all knew what Lent was about ... the fasting rules (8
ounces morning, 2 ounces evening, or *vice versa*), and no
dancing in the ballrooms of romance (except on Patrick's
night). Again, whatever the season, no dancing after mid-
night in some dioceses – making the diocesan boundary a
frontier of hell or heaven. And hell was a very present reality, the ultimate penalty if you committed a mortal sin –

like missing Mass, or dancing at the wrong time, or breaking the fast, or mixed bathing, or company-keeping ...

I still remember the look of horror on the face of a young
Catholic *savant* from France when he heard all this. Were
we all children? Where were our intellectuals, our Catholic
writers and artists, our philosophers and theologians?

Well, yes! we had poets and novelists, and a playwright or
two, but several of them were in exile, or at least in the in-
ternal exile of censorship and the unofficial black-list. And
again public opinion seemed to support the injustice done
to these men and women, for their own good of course,
and our protection and defence.

The Defenders
Catholicism worldwide had indeed gone on the defensive
in the early nineteenth century, in the aftermath of the
Enlightenment and the French Revolution, to protect the
faithful against the dangers of the democratic age. Later,
defence became more 'positive', more militant if you like,
seizing the missionary opportunities of the new era, but
also creating bunkers, safe houses, where Catholic life
could be led in full: Catholic schools and social organisations and sports clubs; Catholic halls for music and drama;
Catholic journals and newspapers; Catholic trades unions
and political parties.

In post-emancipation Ireland too the watchwords were
defence and protection, first against evangelisers and
soupers and tithe-gatherers, later against liberals and an-
archists and secret societies. But there was also the fight,
often heroically fought in the church's name, against
famine and disease and ignorance and poverty and such
forms of injustice as could be tackled within the law. There
were the new slums of the post-famine cities. There was

vice and violence. The church co-operated with secular authority and secular institutions when deemed appropriate, but always preferred Catholic solutions to Catholic problems.

Still, as the twentieth century brought no diminution of the all-pervasive culture of the majority, there appeared to be no need here for specifically Catholic political parties or trades unions. Even the 'secular' National University of Ireland was considered safe for the higher education of Catholic youth.

In the voluntary sector, however, there has been no shortage of confessional organisations, ranging from the Catholic Young Men's Society, now mainly moribund, to the Catholic Boy Scouts, to the Knights of St Columbanus and Opus Dei – still flourishing, as are the Legion of Mary and the Society of St Vincent de Paul, whose immense charitable work has adapted admirably to social change. Another outstanding charity is *Trócaire* which has pioneered work in what we used to call the Third World, and has been joined by other church-inspired groups in the same field. In this new-style missionary activity it would be difficult to identify any trace of defensiveness.

It came as someting of a surprise then to read a recent headline in the weekly *Irish Catholic* telling us how to recognise anti-Catholicism. I had hardly realised such a creature existed any more this side of the wilder slopes of Paisleyite rhetoric. Indeed, as our contributor Gerry Myers remarks, 'it is not so much that people want to criticise the church ... they simply couldn't be bothered.'

But Irish Catholic culture, or what is sometimes called the Irish Catholic mentality, does come in for a fair amount of negative criticism, mainly on the grounds of alleged anti-intellectualism, philistinism and puritanism: in effect, a narrow prejudiced way of looking at life. If this is a fair judgement, and few of us can honestly doubt that there is a grain of truth in it, where does it come from? It is hardly to be seen as arising from the faith itself, from the gospel of Jesus, or from the great tradition which inspired so much of the human and humanist achievement of our civilisation.

Do we then look nearer home for an explanation? Are the roots of the trouble to be found in our history? It was once fashionable to blame our negative qualities on Jansenist influences, which allegedly infected the thinking and teaching of Maynooth College in its early days, imported by 'scholarly French divines'. I don't believe the theory stands up to serious analysis. Victorian pietism and 're-spectability', which did undoubtedly affect middle-class manners and customs here in the last century, have also been blamed; their contribution can hardly be denied, but it is hardly a sufficient explanation. Perhaps, it has been suggested, there has always been a dualism in our outlook: our delight in the mind and the flesh too often clouded by fear. And if so, why here especially?

Impoverishment
In introducing this whole subject of our religious culture which I described as 'unique', I noted its impoverishment caused by the obscurantist philistinism of both secular and regular authority. A slow impoverishment, I said, but one I could add that has quickened considerably over the past two hundred years. I would not wish to idealise the older Gaelic religious tradition, because for one thing we don't have a complete picture of it, and also because the past always looks better at a distance! But, in what we can glean from what was written down, and has been collated and analysed by those competent to do so, there emerges a pic-

ture of a way of life and thought that was aware of the
dark side of humanity and of the world, but not obsessed
by it, that faced creation with open eyes and heart and
mind, and took delight in being part of that creation. It
was, I believe, an essentially 'social' way, comfortable with
people and music and books and the other-world of the
imagination – but comfortable also in solitude or exile,
'alone with none but thee, my God'. It's all there in the
poetry, from the lyrics of the seventh-century monks, down
to the fragments collected by Hyde at the Connacht fire-
sides of a hundred years ago.

The fact that so much was lost or forgotten or abandoned
when the Irish language was abandoned is a matter for
deep regret and shame. And it was, as I have said, an impoverishment of our religious culture, which gradually
became thinner and more threadbare, and so of the humanity of the church, of God's people in a changing Ireland.

This impoverishment has, I believe, been crucial to the development of our present situation, where 'the majority of
people' in places like where Carol Dorgan lives and works
'don't go to Mass', where religion among the young has
come to be seen as 'something that you grow out of', to
quote Anne Looney again, and where in their families 'religion doesn't figure'. Our second essayist, Gerry Myers,
who has considerable experience in working among
young people as well as their elders, has come to the con-
clusion that many (most?) of them

> do not see the church as having any significant part
> to play as they go about the task of sorting through
> the issues, problems and crises of life ...

It would clearly be an oversimplification to ascribe this
state of affairs solely or even mainly to the inner deteriora-

tion of our religious culture. For the radical changes which have since mid-century, but especially in the last thirty-five years or so, changed the face of Irish society, have amounted to nothing less than a cultural revolution which has turned the Irish way of life upside down.

New Departures

It was, I believe, Professor Feichín Ó Dochartaigh, who first used the words 'cultural revolution' in an Irish context. Writing in *Studies* in 1963, he referred to 'great and far-reaching processes within the material culture which inevitably will have great and far-reaching effects in other dimensions of the culture, have already had such effects.'

He was unusually percipient in reading the signs of the times: television had in 1963 barely entered Irish life, our membership of the Common Market (now the European Union) was still ten years in the future, Northern Ireland was still 'peaceful', and the women of Ireland appeared to maintain what someone has called 'their age-long docility'. Soon all these things changed, and more: socio-economic developments established new standards of living to be enjoyed or at least aspired to; the move to a more urban society became definitive, despite (or perhaps because of) new modes of agricultural efficiency and prosperity; free second-level education became widely available.

A range of new departures in public communications have had considerable cultural and social effect. In the electronic media, ever-widening choice in television and video has extended the acceptable frontiers of public discourse and made a nonsense of censorship and related restrictive measures; the same is true of the world of the internet and 'virtual reality' whose ultimate implications can as yet only be guessed at. Public and private transport have brought Irish men and women into corners of the global village hitherto seen as out of range. And wide-ranging mobility of employment is now a commonplace.

Already in the sixties, another radical cultural development was in train elsewhere: the 'sexual revolution' with its vision of freedom unbound by custom or taboo. This too crossed the Irish sea, if a little more slowly. The indispensible agent of the new freedom, a simple, reasonably reliable method of contraception, did however finally become accessible here and has been widely and happily accepted, to be used with varying degrees of responsibility in relationships ranging from the one-night stand to 'traditional' marriage.

But the whole view of *relationship* has been subject to change, some would say mortal damage. The idea of permanence in any state of life has become ever less realistic in a society where the 'job for life' is rapidly becoming an anachronism, as technology and market fluctuation have all but obliterated the familiar contours of employment. Only a minority of young adults can plan for the future with any confidence.

In the absence of statistical evidence, it is difficult to say to what extent marriage is still a preferred option, but the word 'partner' – unheard of in this context only a few years ago – appears more and more often in the social discourse of all classes in Irish society, to the extent that one has heard devout 'conventional' middle-aged parents thanking God that the son or daughter has finally settled into what appears to be a 'stable relationship'. This is by no means universal but, as I say, without facts and figures we can only guess, and my guess would be that marriage as we have known it for so long is becoming one of the victims of the decline of our religious culture.

It may also be the case that the factors which have contributed to the destabilising of marriage and the family –

long regarded as rock-solid pillars of Irish society – have also extended their influence to a reluctance among young people to engage in any longterm commitment, notably that of the ordained ministry or the religious life.

The first and final vocation
Which must finally bring us back to religion itself, to faith, to the church. For Catholics, the proceedings of the Second Vatican Council seemed to promise an age of renewal, not for Catholics alone but for all Christians and indeed all men and women of good will. This promise has been fulfilled, I fear, only on a limited scale, and that mainly in the interior life of the church. I remember Hans Kung remarking of one of the Council's more positive enactments that it was indeed splendid but that it came too late. And then he added, 'Except perhaps for Ireland' – for, as he explained, the Christian life was still strong and vibrant there.

Was he mistaken? The Council did of course bring about much change here, more than at first we realised. Apart from liturgical reform, the introduction of vernacular rites, and the encouragement of a new spirit of fellowship between the Christian churches – with real if limited social benefit in inter-communal relationships in the North, where bad might have been much worse – perhaps the most significant consequence was the new moral emphasis on social justice at home and abroad.

But it has to be said that whatever the reactions, negative or positive, of the generation which came to maturity in the sixties, to subsequent generations the Council is merely part of church history, of only the vaguest significance. So did it come too late here too?

Be that as it may, it is probably more useful for us to consider, however belatedly, how we can bring renewal to life and sustain it among our children. Our four contributors discuss this challenge as a matter of urgency, and while their responses come from different points of departure, they share much common ground. There is a common expression of the need for a new prophetic ministry which will read the signs of the times with an unblinkered eye, and will proclaim the truth with clarity and courage. Gerry Myers stresses the urgency of this need as a ministry in counterpoint to, but preferably not in conflict with, that of priesthood. Carol Dorgan, returning again and again to the *purpose* of the church, emphasises its basic function of 'proclaiming the good news to the poor', and points to the justice desk at CORI as an exemplar of this. And in a wide-ranging tour of the horizon, Anne Looney insists that, against all the indications, the new Ireland *needs* the church, that 'the Christian message can help people to make sense of life and the world', that the church *can* deliver this message of hope. But this can be done only if the church knows 'what it is for', when, as she says, 'it stops trying to save itself'.

Carol Dorgan and Gerry Myers place a particular emphasis on spirituality, the 'heart-vision' which lights up our way forward. Myers insists that 'even on the margins, a type of spirituality is at play in people's lives'. It seems, however, to be but little related to whatever experience they have of church. And yet the church is meant to be the great sign of the Spirit. As Christ is the sacrament of God, so the church is the sacrament of Christ in and for the world. This is ultimately 'what it is for...'

While Myers accepts that what we know as the sacraments (in the plural) are the 'pre-eminent' way in which the church's sacramentality is achieved, there are other ways. Our fourth contributor, Fr Séamus Ryan, is all too aware of the dangers of a priesthood which stands at a distance from the people, however well-equipped for a ministry of 'doing things' for them, but less proficient 'in the more demanding skills required in being a fellow-pilgrim, particularly over rough terrain'.

Recalling the emphasis placed by Vatican II on the church as communion, he sees the role of the priest in making Christ present in the world as centring on the task of enabling communion to grow, and especially through the ministry of healing. This healing of broken people and of broken relationships is a ministry to which all of us are called.

> We are all wounded healers, fragile and sinful, needing just as much care as those we care for. Recent events in the Irish church have borne out this truth.

Thus, in an age of change, a time of 'crisis in vocations', this is the first and final vocation, not to be ignored or 'left to the priest'. It is, after all, His church – and ours.

Disappearing Echoes, New Voices and the Sound of Silence

Anne Looney

This year it finally happened. I knew it was on its way. The signs had been there for some time. Since I began teaching religion in a secondary school, I knew that one day the inevitable would happen. But while I was half expecting it, I was still unprepared for its sudden arrival.

I had planned a lesson about Lent and its origin and meaning in the world of today for a group of post-junior certificate students. A typical class group. Nothing extraordinary about them. Nothing to indicate what was about to happen. No signs. No portents.

The lesson began with a prayer. The students sat down, waiting. 'Lent', I began, 'who can tell me something about Lent?' Now I'll admit to more creative openings but it was the end of a long hard day. I wrote the word 'Lent' on the board. And I waited, chalk in hand, in anticipation of a well-constructed spider diagram filled with words and concepts. The silence that greeted my question should have set the alarm bells ringing. But I put it down to the fact that these were senior students who always needed a bit of prodding. 'What happens during Lent?' I prompted, going for a more phenomenological approach. Silence still. Now this was not the silence that means we just couldn't be bothered answering this question – and believe me such silences do exist. This seemed to be a genuinely *puzzled* silence.

At last. A hand raised. An eager 'yes?' from me, chalk at ready. '*Trócaire* boxes,' the student said. I grasped at those two words and wrote them carefully on the board and drew a line between these new words and the lonely *Lent* in the centre of the board. But I was sure that the breakthrough had been made. I forged ahead. 'And why do we have *Trócaire* boxes in Lent?' I pressed, preparing to write the word *fasting* on the board. 'Because no-one has any money at Christmas,' came the response. I wanted to laugh. But only briefly.

Further investigation by me did produce 'Ash Wednesday' and 'giving up things when you were a kid'. But that was it. And that is when it happened. The new Ireland arrived to take a seat in my classroom. The new Ireland had had its foot in the door for some time. I knew that sacramental attendance was low, decreasing as the students moved through the school. Some of the students had not been inside a church, apart from school liturgies, since their confirmations. But it was still difficult to see this new Ireland creeping in the door. It was easy to ignore it in the face of the continuing interest in the person of Jesus, in all forms of prayer, in the mystery of God and in issues of justice and peace. Plenty there to be getting on with.

But slowly and stealthily the new Ireland had stolen into my classroom and shocked me with its presence on that fateful February day. All of the students had learned about Lent before. In primary school. In the junior cycle of secondary school. Why then did the vast majority of them have almost no recollection of anything to do with Lent? Because it was quite simply not a part of their experience. Neither, for the majority, was it part of their families' experience. It just didn't figure.

One of the features of the new Ireland is that religion

doesn't figure. At least not the way it used to, anyway.
There are other distinguishing features of our new culture
worth mentioning. We have new paradigms for success –
most of them economic. We have new heroes and heroines,
transient creatures who come into fashion as quickly as
they leave it. We have new forms of communication. And
we have new communication problems between parents
and children and between children and children. We have
new uncertainties in working life and in relationships. We
are a changed people living in a changed place. People like
to remember with fondness those days of leaving the key
in the door and the family fortune on the dresser. They remember pushing black bicycles to cross-roads dances or
taking buses to ballrooms of romance. They remember
how it was all much simpler and, most of all, much more
certain. Someone once said that the great certainties were
the GAA, the Catholic church and the Fianna Fáil party.
(Although not necessarily in that order!) 'One has sold its
soul to corporate boxes, one is in disarray and one has
been replaced by a rainbow coalition!' The old certainties
are gone! All is changed, changed utterly. We are indeed a
changed people living in a changed place. Or rather we are
a changing people living in a changing place. For it is the
pace of change that disturbs people as much as the results
of change. When fifth and sixth year students remark on
the behaviour of first year students and say that it was different in their day, we know that the pace of change is fast.
Frighteningly fast.

Cultural Atheism

During the transitional period from old certainties to the
new Ireland it seems that we passed through a phase of
grey areas. Nostalgia grew for the old certainties, for the
old black and white world, and the 'new' religious education in schools came in for a bit of a bashing. Those of us
involved in the teaching of religion were often blamed for

creating these grey areas. We were not, apparently, teaching the basics, the ten commandments, sin and punishment; we weren't telling children that not going to Mass on Sundays was a sin. If we were teaching them this, then they would all be going gladly, not complaining that it was boring! During these grey days, if anyone had asked, religion teachers would have confirmed that all of the basics were being duly delivered, but that they were no longer *culturally* supported. They could have pointed out, for example, that while they were trying to teach that the eucharist was the peak and summit of Christian life and worship, Sunday morning was being targeted as a prime time for music television for young teenagers. They could have pointed out that while they were teaching that neighbours should be loved, the nation was busy building walls and installing burglar alarms. But that was the eighties.

These are the nineties. And the new Ireland is here to stay. And Lent doesn't matter. Religion doesn't matter. For some at least. And the numbers are growing. On paper, Irish Catholicism looks fine. Sacramental attendance remains the highest in western Europe and among the highest in the world. An endless number of surveys show that we still believe in God, in an afterlife and in the power of prayer. And most Catholic families still baptise their babies, bring their eight year olds for first communion and their pre-teens to kneel at the feet of a bishop for confirmation. Of course there have been the series of scandals, the mistakes, the poor public relations, but there is a feeling that it's better all out in the open now. This 'openness' is perceived as a sign of health. A sign of renewed strength and vigour. And so it may well be. On paper at least.

But a closer look will reveal that it is now possible to live a life in Ireland, especially in some parts of Ireland and within some socio-economic groups, untouched by institutional religion. It's not so much a matter of ideological, as a sort of *cultural* atheism. In the past Catholicism in Ireland was a cultural phenomenon. Irish Catholicism wasn't just handed on from generation to generation. It was *inhaled*. It was in the air, in the pattern of everyday living and dying. Ask some of the adults who no longer practise their religion about the reasons why. The vast majority are puzzled by the question. They just ... *stopped*. Irish Catholicism is now seen as something that you grow out of. It's something for children, and for many, confirmation has become the sacrament of farewell rather than the completion of initiation. We give them memories of a great day, money in the post office and little else.

We certainly give them little experience of Lent, as I found out. Now my class on Lent continued after the initial trauma. I taught them about the season and its origins. They learned about the catechumenate (and all said that it would be better to baptise babies rather than adults because it would be too *embarrassing* for adults), and about penance and sackcloth and ashes. They were surprised to hear where Mardi Gras came from, and carnival and all those other lenten terms. When the bell went for the end of class they knew more about Lent than they did at the beginning. But as they and the new Ireland left school that day and clambered aboard the bus for the post modern world, I suspected that Lent really meant as little to them as it had the moment I wrote the word on the board.

Whispering Echoes and Booming Tones
All of which left me, and continues to leave me, with something of a catechetical dilemma. Now this dilemma has been around for a while but is becoming increasingly urgent. Catechesis, I was told in the early days of my training, is about the process of bringing people to maturity of faith. The word *catechesis* comes from a word meaning to

echo. It happens within the context of a community of faith. It must. For if it is to be based on an echoing, then the catechetical voice cannot be the only one. The participants in the catechetical process must be surrounded by echoes of belief and commitment for a true dialogue to take place. The catechist should not be a Baptist-like figure crying in the wilderness. In fact, I learned, school catechesis is only one element of the church's catechetical mission. The sounds made in school should be supported by echoes made at home and in the parish. There should be a harmony of catechetical echoing so that, in theory, the message delivered about Lent should be reinforced by messages received at home and in the parish.

But these students have no connection with their parishes and most of their homes are Lenten-free zones. Echoes of Lent may be picked up from billboards advertising the *Trócaire* campaign. But the rest is silence. Which makes a mockery of the school catechetical enterprise. There is no harmony of catechetical echoing. In fact the voices heard outside the religion classroom are often in complete discord with those heard inside it. With all the innovative teaching in the world, the voice of school catechesis and any echoes which may resonate from it are drowned out by the cacophony of cultural indifference. Schools cannot carry the church's catechetical mission single handedly. They never could. There was, up to several years ago, a tacit acceptance that it could 'be left to the schools'. But in a culture of disappearing echoes, classes like my lenten one will become increasingly common. As echoes of cultural Catholicism become whispers, those of us who have committed ourselves to the church in its catechetical mission, or indeed in any way, strain our ears for new voices, hopeful voices, strong voices, voices of faith for the new Ireland.

But we have to listen very hard.

It's a strange thing to say, but it's a long time since I have heard the church preach authentically about anything. For an institution that's about the business of good news, this is a damning indictment. And I say it with regret rather than recrimination. I want the church to speak and preach, I want its voice to be heard. As a teacher of religion, I know that the effectiveness of my enterprise depends on this. I have heard voices of individuals within the church attempt to set the culture echoing with resonances of meaning for the new Ireland. I was in the audience at the now notorious *Late Late Show* that gave the first public airing to some of these voices. Voices that wouldn't be silenced. Voices that won't be silenced. Voices of people who believe passionately in the church and the possibilities it offers to the world. And did those voices find echoes? In every pub, supermarket and street corner these voices were the subject of analysis, discussion and comment. The new Ireland had heard brief snatches of new voices. When will we hear the likes again? Therein lies the problem. These new voices are lost in the booming tones of official churchdom. As the people of God, some of us are not very good at listening to each other. Selective deafness is an affliction of the Irish church.

Voices of Reason
And some might also accuse it of selective dumbness. In the Ireland which is building itself around us, church voices, and the good news they should bring, are often absent. Silent. Interestingly, one area of cultural life where the church continues to create authentic and resonating echoes is the area of socio-economic debate and critique. I wonder why this is so. It seems to be the only part of life in which the church is preaching rather than responding, teaching rather than defending. The voice of the Conference of Religious in Ireland – CORI – specifically that of Fr Sean Healy and Sr Brigid Reynolds, is one given serious consid-

eration in the new Ireland. Why? Because this is a voice
that takes the new Ireland seriously, that listens to the new
Ireland. It begins in economic and social realities experienced by everyone and is not afraid to engage in a critique
that offers new possibilities. And this critique is imbued
with gospel principles and rooted in the social teaching of
the church. The voice of CORI is a consistent and persist-
ent one; its witness credible and authentic. It is perhaps the
only official church voice given any credibility by the
media. No economic debate is complete without the voice
of CORI. If only the church could find similar voices for
other areas of life. But again, the rest is silence.

But what kind of voices do we need? What should the
church be saying in and to the new Ireland? One thing is
certain. New voices must be voices of *reason*. For this, despite appearances at times, is a rational age. As a nation we
are more educated than we ever have been. We have access to information, to ideas, to debates that were never
dreamed of by the people pushing the black bicycles! One
thing that always strikes me about the voice of CORI is its
reasonableness. Other voices are not demonised and dis-
missed as destructive of society. They are listened to, heard
and addressed. I always associate the voice of CORI in
economic debate with the phrase 'but there is an alternative'. During the run-up to the divorce referendum, there
was a shortage of reasonable voices. Now the church was
not the only guilty party in this regard. But for an institution that teaches that a well-informed conscience should
be the foundation for decision making, the church offered
little in the way of reason. John Bruton, in an interview at
the time of the referendum, suggested that every yes voter
had a no voter inside, and every no voter had a yes voter
inside. I think that most would agree with his analysis. It
was a confusing time. And people who grew up in an age of
black and white looked for reason. They got disappearing

daddies, drunk drivers, shredded societal fabric, juvenile delinquency, bankruptcy, helpless women and predatory men. And the threat of sacramental sanctions! Now not all of these gems came from church voices, but it strikes me that at a time when people wanted to hear about the vision of Christian marriage, about the sacrament of life-long commitment, when they wanted to hear a *reasonable* voice, such a voice was absent. As long as the voice of reason is not heard, it seems that people will still feel that religion doesn't matter.

But of course religion does matter to some. It matters a great deal. At parent teacher meetings, I meet some who are genuinely concerned to hand on a living faith to their children. I meet fellow parishioners who want to make the local Christian community an attractive one, a community that stands for something. Somehow, I feel that the commitment of these adults, and young adults, is taken for granted. For such commitment is not easily made in the current climate. And yet parish committees, councils and core groups continue to form, usually, it must be said, drawing on the same cohort who run the guides and the residents' association. How does the church support those adults who remain committed to it through thick and thin? What voice addresses them? Addresses us? Addresses me?

The Hungry Sheep
Because the church has invested so heavily in the education of children and young people, the education of adults has been largely neglected. The church has, for the most part, left its adult members with the religion they were given in school. The questions and answers that formed the core of the religious education of several generations were, it seemed, the ones they would need in later life. The 'new' religious education received by later generations brought them, it was believed, to maturity of faith at eight-

een. The church saw to it that such an education was delivered … which was to see them through young adulthood,
parenthood, middle age and beyond, at a time of the most
rapid cultural change ever experienced by a generation of
Irish men and women. Very little else was offered. That
was it. Religious education was for children and young
people. This was what the church voice seemed to be saying. And now, when parishes provide talks for Lent, or
short courses in scripture, there is usually disappointment
at the numbers who show up. 'The same few' is generally
the complaint of course organisers. Is it surprising?

Adult religious education is not for the faint-hearted. And
that applies to leaders and participants. People's life experience has to be taken seriously. Nothing can be taken at face
value. Those participants who are living through this time
of change, who are ageing as the new Ireland is being born
around them, bring important questions to the catechetical
process. They desire maturity of faith, but know that they
are embarking on a lifelong quest. But the voice of adult
religious education in Ireland is almost a whisper.

A few years ago I was in another classroom when a different catechetical bombshell was dropped. Not the arrival of
the new Ireland, for that was embodied in the students,
but the interruption of a church voice which said *stop*. I
was involved with an adult religious education project
called *Foundation in Faith for Adults*. It began in the autumn of
1988 and in deference to the world footballing authorities
was given the acronym FIFA! It was sponsored by the
Dublin Institute of Adult Education and organised by
some of the staff of the institute and a team of tutors. It
began simply. People were sent by their parishes to one of
two centres for a year-long course. The course was made
up of three eight-week modules. The modules were on
scripture, morality, ecclesiology, christology and other top-
ics. These were not formal lectures, but two-hour sessions

which combined a variety of methods drawing heavily on the participants' own experiences and questions.

People came from different parishes and from different backgrounds. The group which began in 1988 stayed for three years! People came and went from the group during that time as their own life patterns changed, but a core remained for three years. By the time they had finished, the two centres had turned into six, and a network of FIFA groups had been established. I began working with another group which was well into its third module when the bomb dropped. It dropped on a Monday afternoon. This I remember all too well because the group was meeting on a Monday night and had to be told that when the module was finished, there would be no more. The Dublin Institute of Adult Education would not be offering any more religious education. This group of adults, and the other groups meeting around Dublin, were to meet no longer. Breaking this news to the group was one of the most distressing experiences of my life. I had represented the voice of reasoning faith to them. We had been working together to make sense of the nature and purpose of church. Now I felt we were being let down by that church. Badly let down.

The Dublin Institute of Adult Education continues to exist. It offers courses in business(!) and runs a mothers' group for the inner city of Dublin. But it offers no more adult religious education. For, we were told, financial restructuring reasons. Some of the staff involved continue to work in adult faith formation independently of the institute. But FIFA is no more. I often wonder where it is? All those session plans and resources drawn out of the experience of so many adults? Are they on a shelf somewhere with the programmes put together by the Mount Oliver Institute in Dundalk, and courses organised in the Diocesan Centre in Galway? All now closed.

It seems that at a time when people need to hear a voice of
reason, when they need help to make sense of cultural
change, when they need support in the handing on of faith
to their children, when commitment cannot be taken for
granted but must be nurtured, when people search for that
maturity of faith which catechesis is supposed to offer
them, 'the hungry sheep look up and are not fed'. Most of
them anyway. For some there is the option of third level
study of theology. For many there is starvation.

Hope Deferred

New voices must also be voices of *imagination*. Imagination
has been sorely lacking in the Irish church of late. Imagination is the power to read and create symbols. It is the
power to see possibilities, to offer solutions, to re-order
priorities when necessary. Imagination is a risky business.
I was born during Vatican II. It has always struck me that
many of the documents represent a great act of imagination on the part of participants. Enormous risks were taken.
By individuals and by the Council itself. *Gaudium at Spes* in
particular took the enormous risk of applying that imagination to 'the signs of the times'. Imagination belongs to the
realm of dreams and visions. What might a voice of imagination say to the Irish context?

It might offer new pastoral possibilities beyond the parish
structure. It might speak of new forms of liturgical participation. It might dare to say that we need to explore our understanding of sacraments and of their celebration, not
least with children. A voice of imagination could live with
a plurality of ideas and expressions, seeing that the Holy
Spirit is a gift to the whole church and not just its leadership. A voice of imagination might call for a look at the
business of school-based catechesis and its meaning in the
context of the new Ireland. And a voice of imagination
might call for the empowerment of people so that they

might be agents of culture rather than its victims. True imagination doesn't try to hide behind public relations strategies. It gets straight to the heart of the matter. The voice of imagination speaks first. It doesn't wait to be questioned, or forced out of its silence. I have heard it said that the Irish church is suffering from an image problem. It isn't. It is suffering from an imagination problem.

The new Ireland calls for the church to speak in a voice of *hope*. And in some cases it does this quite well. Its voice is heard on the side of the marginalised, and, among the casualties of this new and fast-paced culture of ours, there are voices of hope for the culturally weakened. But now there is a need to bring hope to the spiritually weakened. In the church today, somewhere between the committed and the lost, there are the bewildered. They want to believe. They want to belong. But they are confused. They are hurt. They may have years of loyalty to a church they feel has let them down badly. Their hurt and confusion is given little place for expression.

Some have stopped contributing financially. This could be described as a petty reaction, but for the generation who grew up on the 'pay-pray-obey' model of church, it is the only private and public gesture they have the power to make. Theirs is a simmering anger and a deep-rooted disappointment. Voices of hope *are* beginning to speak, but not directly to them. Something is wrong. What they hear may be focused on institutional survival rather than on the service of the people of God. There seems to be a sense that the church needs defending, a sense that the wagons should be put in a circle against the arrows of the enemy. The trouble is that the circle of wagons has also shut out the vast majority of committed believers who feel the same arrows when they pick up a newspaper with the latest scandal, or they tune into the latest documentary on television. And it is these wounded and bewildered people who desperately need to hear the voice of hope – above the din of the attacking Indians.

Meanwhile ...

Meanwhile, back in the classroom where no one can re-member an experience of Lent, the teacher must carry on. But what is to be done when the other voices are not to be heard or are reduced to whispers lost on winds of cultural indifference? Many teachers of religion work valiantly at filling the gap. They organise lenten fasts and use the ex-ploration of the experience of fasting as a way of teaching the value of Lent. Similarly, they organise school liturgies in the full knowledge that such celebrations may be the only contact the student has with the sacramental life of the church. And we can continue like this, but we know that in the context of the new Ireland, maturity of faith be-comes an increasingly elusive goal.

The religion classroom will shortly be offered the sound of a new voice – the possibility of syllabuses for Junior and Leaving Certificate Religious Education from the Depart-ment of Education rather than from the churches, and with the possibility of assessment and certification. These syllabuses (as yet in their draft form) arise out of the stated aim of providing for the *holistic* education of the individual in his/her social and cultural contexts. The introduction to the drafts says that in order to understand Irish culture it is necessary to understand the Christian traditions and be exposed to the variety of religious traditions and the non-religious interpretations of life. This development in sec-ond level education will force the debate about the nature and purpose of religious education in schools. It will force questions about the viability of school-based catechesis in the new cultural context. And it is a question that won't go away.

I am convinced that the cultural context of the new Ireland that arrived so suddenly in my classroom on that February day *needs* the church. I believe that the Christian message can help people of all ages to make sense of life and of the world, can offer the imagination needed to envisage a better world, and the hope necessary to make that vision a reality. I continue to believe that the Irish church can deliver this saving message. But only when it stops trying to save itself.

Sign and Reality: Searching for the Sacramentality of the Church

Gerry Myers

I begin this chapter with an 'I' statement, which I suppose befits a psychotherapist. In my own life I found my holy place, and it is not where you might expect. It is not a church or a shrine, but it is a magical place near Spanish Point in County Clare where the rocks and the sea weave together a long thread of wild coastline. Here, on my own and with others, I have experienced church and I have experienced my God.

I am reflecting here on my personal experience as a Roman Catholic, as well as on working with others. As you will gather, I'm somebody who is much more at home on the margins than at the centre. I suspect that the Catholic centre may not recognise itself in what I write, but I would hope that a lot of people may see their own familiar face in it.

I work in private practice, and I use a humanistic and integrative approach. This approach is a comfortable one when dealing with a whole range of emotions, beliefs, sensations, cognitions and behaviours and it's well tuned to the religious and spiritual dimension of people's lives. Indeed some of the literature of humanistic and integrative psychotherapy is shared with Christian spirituality; the writings of Kierkegaard, for example, and of Frankl.

In my present work, I encounter a wide variety of human problems, and I often find that in attempting to sort them out the spiritual dimension of life plays a major part. In fact *some* problems are resolved only when handled in an explicitly religious or spiritual way. But just as I am surprised at the frequency with which the spiritual presents itself in therapy, I am equally surprised at the rarity with which reference is made to the *church*, even by the most solid of Irish Catholics.

In many ways this ties in with my experience in other types of work. For fifteen years I was a member of a religious congregation specialising in education and youthwork, including five years with university students. During all those years young people often got into debate with me about a range of 'church' issues – priests' cars and houses, contraception and premarital sex, married priests and woman priests – *but in dealing with problems in their personal lives the church seemed to impinge little enough.* It was clear that these young people thought of the church as 'out there' somewhere, and cut off from them and their lives, and this despite the fact that some of them were Sunday Mass-goers. The point I am making here is that many of the people I have worked with, in a variety of roles, do not seem to see the church as having any significant part to play as they go about the task of sorting through the issues, problems, and crises of life (of youth, of middle age, of growing old).

'Spirituality' now
I believe, however, that *spirituality*, understood broadly, is alive and well and living in Ireland. I suppose that by spirituality I mean that people – adults as well as younger men and women – subscribe to something meaningful, deeper, higher and larger than self; something or someone of transcendent value and worthy of being 'believed in'. I don't necessarily mean that this spirituality is focused on God, or that we might even consider it a 'good' spirituality, although it often is. Some years ago I was working in un-

structured youthwork on the 'margins'. Many of the teenagers I was dealing with were 'on the wild side': frequently in trouble with the law, rarely at school, virtually certain to have parented a child before they were eighteen. But many of these kids were able to work through many of their life crises with a strong attention to values which were important to them: values like loyalty, love, and integrity. Admittedly some of these teenagers were also well able to subscribe to the 'spirituality', if you like, of people like Kurt Cobain, an altogether darker and more hopeless view of the world. The point is that even on the margins, a type of 'spirituality' is at play in people's lives.

Spirituality often displays itself most clearly in a crisis. In its Christian and Catholic form, spirituality comes into its own at the death of a spouse, family member, or friend. Here personal and communal faith and ritual flow in a deep meaningfulness which matches the enormity of the event of death. And even in the trauma of the post-funeral period this spirituality can be very much to the fore. The man who has lost his wife in a fatal car crash may curse the supposedly loving God, he may demand to know how God could have permitted the crash and, virtually looking God in the eye, he may say that, if God can allow such a tragedy, maybe there is no God at all. Here the man's apparently negative spirituality is flowing like a well-oiled machine. Indeed in therapy one often hears faith-full anger directed vehemently at God. Similarly, a woman struggling with the sudden discovery that the long-standing marriage which she had thought to be deep, intimate and secure was in fact full of cracks and deep deceits, will probably feel the pull between trust and mistrust. She had trusted that her relationship was as it seemed, but now experiences the way sheer deceit challenges that trust. And yet this woman, in that very crisis, may well choose to subscribe, even still, to a faith in the fundamental 'trustability' of life because that is what her spirituality suggests to her. In this sense the woman is sorting out an issue in favour of a belief in a larger and more trustworthy dimension of life. She may well express this basic trust in religious terms such as 'God will stand by me', or she may not, but in any case the basic trust still arises in her own spirit, and is in that sense part of her spirituality.

Again, a young man suffering in a black depression about his poor education, lack of relationships and poor employment prospects, may find a way forward for himself, not in Prozac, but in bringing before himself the things he values deeply. In a crisis of depression he may rediscover the value of *care* and may lift his own spirits by acting in favour of that value, by doing something positive, something 'social', like working with the Simon Community or even setting up a youth club. What I am saying, then, is that in a *crisis* a person's underlying spirituality, worldview, call it what you will, often comes to the fore. This spirituality may not be specifically Christian, but it will be real, and this psychotherapist meets it frequently!

It is not, of course, universally the case. There are also many people who work out their life crises and issues with reference only to the demands of the moment, and using only 'average everydayness', to quote Heidegger, as their benchmark. In fact for such people such checking of themselves against the benchmark of the herd often *is* their crisis, or if you like, their neurosis.

Church on the margins
But meeting spirituality as often as I do, it amazes me that the church seems to play such a marginal role. For in crisis situations what is truly central comes to the fore, and what is marginal is left out. In the life crises I have worked with, spirituality is often central, and church seems to be more

marginal. Let me say a little more about this. When I was in my late teens I took part in a training programme for mountain leadership. We learned a lot about handling emergencies, about keeping our head and about following sensible, worked-out procedures. That was in the classroom! The real test came on the night hike when the little marker stick you were looking for on a strange, freezing mountain at 4.00 a.m. wasn't where you expected it to be! In that crisis situation you quickly found out which skills were core and which were marginal. Crises are a great way of finding out just where you are at, and crises are the stock-in-trade of my job.

Going back to the man who had lost his wife in a car crash. At the time of her death, church came to the fore; the church is very good with death. He was comforted by his priest, he was helped with the planning of the church funeral, he heard the sermon and saw the grave being blessed. All of these things were deeply meaningful to him. And church still has a place in his life. And yet I have sat with many men and women like him who, in the years after a bereavement, have not adjusted to their loss, and I can honestly say that in the working out of their bottled-up grief church has hardly featured in anything other than a marginal way. There has been passionate rage against God, yes, and that I suppose is spirituality at work, but church has been more incidental.

I am certainly not saying that the church has no place in the lives of people I have worked with. I am aware how deeply many value Sunday Mass and the other sacraments and sacramentals. I am aware of the still widespread (if not altogether unqualified) regard for bishops, priests, nuns and brothers, as for special places of prayer such as shrines, pilgrimages and so on. It is true also that there is considerable respect for what the church says. I personally know many people, mostly old, many middle-aged, some younger, for whom the church is a warm and living bedrock. But there is also a whole body of people for whom the church is on the outer edge of their lives, and others for whom what the church does or says is of little or no consequence at all. In fact I often find that it is not so much that people want to criticise the church; often it is much worse than that, they simply couldn't be bothered – even if they are Mass-goers the church has moved out to the margins of their lives. In crisis situations, the church is so easily cut out of the loop, and that is a key measure of its relevance.

Obviously, there are areas where it is not so easy to cut the church out. In moral dilemmas about sexual behaviour the church has a strong voice which may help young people to resolve the tensions. But this strong voice is often a negative one which finds it difficult to celebrate a fully incarnated sexuality. And, in fact, many life crises are not about such matters at all! It is in these other areas that the church tends to move decidedly towards the margins.

Sacrament and Word
The church, of course, has many roles, a key one of which is to be the sacrament of God's reign in the world. The notion of sacramentality is complex, and among the motifs under which it can be considered are *sign* and *reality*. The church is both the sign of God's redeeming activity in the world, and it is the reality of the activity too; in a sense, the church is both the signpost and the destination.

As the sign and also the presence of God's reign in the world, the church to which we belong has a sign function and a making-present function. What I want to do now, on the basis of having spent twenty years working in a caring role with people, is to ask whether the church performs these functions effectively. And in an unreflected way the answer that comes to me immediately is that it doesn't. But ...

Some weeks ago a grandaunt of mine, aged 101, died. I visited her shortly before the end and, typically, she had a rosary beads in her hand and she was praying. Mass, visits from the local priest, pilgrimages, the Angelus, confession, the Pope's pronouncements, visits from fellow Mass-goers, these had all been central parts of her life up until very recent years. I remember ten years ago, when she was 91 years old, she could give me a vivid description of each of the stained-glass windows in our parish church, and she could talk at length about each of the parish priests, not least the long-reigning Monsignor who effectively was the *Signeur* of our town until he died. The church was at the very centre of her life. And if it signposted and made effective God's presence, then God must have been very present to her indeed!

It would be easy to discuss her experiences as a relic of the past, and in some ways the centrality of the church in her life was a projection of the past into the present, brought about by her longevity. But, and this is important, there are people of all ages of whom the same can be said. There are many people for whom the church is a hearth at which they warm themselves. And there are a great many others who are regular Sunday Mass-goers and who assign an important place to the church in their lives; for these people there are real ways in which the church does make present God's reign in the world.

The sacraments are in effect the pre-eminent way in which the church is itself a sacrament; they are the key way in which the church is most clearly active in people's lives. Sunday Mass, weddings and funerals are, I suppose, the main point of contact with the church. And yet, even in the Ireland of the provinces, there is a change well under way in which Sunday Mass is losing its grip on people. The major sacraments of passage are still widely celebrated, of course, but the church of the sacraments is gradually moving towards the edge of life in Ireland.

And with that comes the gradual loss of other ways in which the church makes real God's presence. The primary way in which God's word is made present is in liturgical and paraliturgical settings. The preaching of the word outside of these settings has, in practice, been the province of Protestant Evangelicals. As liturgical events become less central in people's lives, so too does the hearing of God's word.

Another way in which the church has been involved in making real God's presence in the world has been through what I might call 'works of care'. There are, let it not be forgotten, sisters who are bringing standards of true excellence to residential childcare, there are sisters and brothers working all God's hours on the margins in support of families in distress. There are men and women who translate their church membership into working in support of the lost and depressed in society. In all of these ways the church is expressing its sacramentality.

But herein lies a problem. It is easy to see the priests, nuns and brothers as acting on behalf of the church. But in ever-increasing ways, other people are taking over. Many of the people associated with orphan work in Romania, with care for the Chernobyl victims, with relief of famine in Rwanda, have in fact been 'lay' people. Perhaps they have been motivated by their membership of the church, perhaps not. Unfortunately, the church does not seem to have found a way to take to itself the Christian work of care in society which is undertaken by its ordinary members, work

which thoroughly and effectively brings the values of the
kingdom to fruition in the world. The difficulty seems to
be that this church of ours finds it very hard to take owner-
ship of something it doesn't control.

The church has always seen its teaching role as a central
gift of God to the world; that, in this teaching, God's word
is made present. Scripture, upon which the teaching
should be based, covers the full breadth of human existence. There is a great balance in it; it often has its own cor-
rectives built in. But it is clear that the teachings of the
church, *as they come across in the media*, are focused not on
the whole breadth of human life but usually on sex, repro-
duction, marriage, and the termination of life. I do understand, of course, that this is just what is reported widely in
the popular media, and in fact the church does have things
to say in the wider field of human life. But as reflected in
the media, the church has allowed itself to be *seen* to be
focused on sexual issues, and negatively focused at that.

On this score a memory comes to mind from my days
working in a university. The scene is a young student couple
at a discussion group, he sitting on the floor leaning back
against her legs, she sitting on a chair, her fingers gently
running through his hair. He leans forward to make his
contribution, her hands falling lightly onto his shoulders;
he says, 'You know the church is obsessed with sex.' The
church certainly hasn't found a way to get a positive message on sexuality into a setting like this. The church's
heard voice is too dour, too negative and too legalistic and,
as I have suggested, it seems to have little to say to young
people in the springtime of their sexuality.

Priests, Prophets and Radhaus Square
My own belief is that the church is too *priestly*. By that I
don't mean that there are too many clergy but that there is

too much of a 'priestly' way of thinking, as distinct from a prophetic way of thinking. The priestly way mostly focuses on ritual, law, continuity, orthodoxy, structure, hierarchy and delimited community. These elements are to be found in Old Testament priesthood and, in a changed form, they have found their way into the modern church. But of course the Old Testament also provides us with another 'office', that of prophet. The key contribution that the prophets made was to unmask the truth, to bring a situation into sharp relief, and they were not beyond making the odd spectacular gesture, as Jeremiah did. Certainly they were not afraid to rock the religious boat. Prophets were charismatic figures, often on the margins, usually unpopular (especially with the establishment), filled with passion, and very tuned to the way God's work-of-redemption was being misused in Israel. My own belief is that the role of the prophet has sadly diminished.

It's hard to find clear examples of prophecy at work in the church today. Occasionally, an individual voice may be raised to confront or expose something unacceptable in church or society, or both. But generally what there is of prophecy is tacked on to the tail of some other ministry, and then the prophetic gets lost – often under the weight of the 'priestly'. And when the church *is* actively prophetic, signposting the kingdom of God, it's doing so in a world where there are many competitors. There is a host of 'prophetic' voices about these days, and the church's is by no means the clearest.

As I write this I am on holiday in Copenhagen, and right now I am sitting in the snow-covered Radhaus Square. It is a fascinating, living, unharmonious place. On one side you have the big, sombre, redbrick Radhaus, the Town Hall, and alongside it the equally sombre facade of the Palace Hotel, where I am sitting. Great, solid, dour buildings standing up for history and the coldness of winter;

Kierkegaard might well have formed some of his ideas here. But that is only one side of the square. Much more striking are all the modern buildings which are facades for bright, succinct advertising signs of every colour and shape under the sun. At night time, the scene is amazing: Carlsberg, Agfa, Sodolin, Philips, Nilfisk, all demanding our attention and projecting us into our next consumer decision. Town Hall Square offends our aesthetic sensibilities, the tensions are simply too great! The old dark fortress of rooted tradition sits too uneasily with the bright dynamic world which points onwards and outwards, and yet this place is the heart of this city, its living focus where young and old eventually find themselves. In fact the tension in the aesthetic of the square is also the tension to be found in life, and it is the tension which should be found in the life of the church.

My own belief is that the church has identified too much with the symbol of the old Radhaus building and, where it has tried to operate in the world of signs, it has been too lifeless and ineffective. Perhaps the church could learn something from Philips. In Radhaus Square, under their huge illuminated sign, Philips have two gilt figures. One is a young woman with the umbrella, the other has a bicycle. If rain or snow is expected the young woman with the umbrella pops out, otherwise it is the woman with the bicycle we see. Philips has something very useful to contribute in this Nordic weather-bound country, and it does it well.

If the church is to take up the prophetic role, which is very much a *sign* role, then it must be able to speak to us like the signs in Radhaus Square, not that it must sell something, but that it must point up something to us.

The spiritual dimension needs to be highlighted. These days we are encouraged to see ourselves in *holistic* terms,

being made up of body, mind and spirit. But we are often
at a loss to find the spiritual in ourselves. It may be we
haven't got the words to express it, and often there's a
sense of sailing in uncharted waters.

Design for Life

For many people the difficulty is how to tune to their own
spiritual dimension, and how to form a coherent spirituality
in a world full of half-formed and competing spiritualities
and indeed non-spiritualities. For these people the experience is like being in the Radhaus Square of their spirituality. The church can often be the dour Town Hall, only really
making an effort for people who actually go into it, and
even then speaking more with a priestly rather than a
prophetic voice. What is needed is for the church to discover a bright, dynamic, non-legalistic, prophetic voice
which will usefully address people in the busyness of their
lives, which will give them a map for living or, as A. M.
Hunter once said of the beatitudes, a design for life.

What I have attempted to present in this chapter are some
reflections on the relative peripherality of the church in the
lives of many of the people with whom I have worked. I
have acknowledged that what I have set out may not tie in
with the experience of everybody, but I believe it has a
good fit for many. I am not so much worried about criticism of the church, as that people don't even bother to
criticise. Perhaps the problem is that the church in practice
too easily identifies its sacramentality with 'administer-
ing' the sacraments, and its soul with structures. Certainly
it has vastly undervalued its prophetic side, depriving
people of relevant signposts by which to navigate as they
live their lives in the world *out there*. It may well be that the
sign value of the church might be best seen precisely in
this prophetic function, a function which would not by
any means be the preserve of the clergy. Maybe the Spirit

is sending a prophetic call to people within the church. The challenge to the *priestly* church would be to try and accept the living prophetic word within itself.

I have not set out to slate the church. I have experienced much that is good and valuable within it. But if it is to be deeply meaningful in the lives of people such as the majority of those with whom I work, it will have to move out of the narrow confines within which it lives and move into the maelstrom of this Radhaus Square world. It will have to discover that the effective sign is one that is creative, dynamic, positive, and takes people where they are at. The simple reality is that, increasingly, people are not at church!

The Church:
Foolish Dream or Hope for the Future?

Carol Dorgan

A couple of years ago I happened to go to the Saturday evening vigil Mass in what would be considered an affluent parish in Dublin's south side. Instead of the homily the celebrant spoke of the work of the diocesan charity *Crosscare*, and of how generous the people were last year at the annual collection. Next weekend would be the turn of the collection once again, and since, in the intervening twelve months, the needs which the charity catered for had increased, he encouraged the people to their 'habitual generosity'. Solid and factual – within well-defined limits.

But I had foolishly, perhaps, hoped for something more, and at the end of Mass I left with a familiar feeling of disappointment and frustration. An occasion for a prophetic voice to be raised was lost. It would have been very much to the point, I thought, to ask the question 'Why?' Why was *Crosscare* asking for an increase in donations? Why were more people seeking its help? Why ask for donations yet again? Is there not something more fundamentally askew in society, even more within the diocesan church, when there are brother and sister Christians only a few miles away dependent on food kitchens, food vouchers, second-hand clothes shops, emergency payments and, when all else fails, the instinct for survival? Would this have been too risky a question to raise in a wealthy area? Would it have been too 'political'? Was there, perhaps, a fear that some people would leave and go to another parish to find a more 'comfortable' message? I suspect that

such questions had never occurred to the priest; that he
saw no way to link his personal faith with wider social
issues; that for him, as for most of us, religion had always
been presented as a private matter between himself and
God; not a life-involving relationship, but rather a life-
transcending or life-avoiding one.

I have reflected on this experience many times since, noting
how crowded that suburban church was in comparison
with the parish where I live and worship, and putting this
beside the words of Jesus when asked by John's disciples if
he really were the 'one who is to come'. Jesus answered:
'Go back and tell John what you have seen and heard: the
blind see again, the lame walk, lepers are cleansed and the
deaf hear, the dead are raised to life and the good news is
proclaimed to the poor, and happy is the one who does not
lose faith in me' (Lk 7:22).

The Question
What is the church *for*? This is the question. Is it for maintaining the crowds in middle class parishes, ensuring that
the sacraments get celebrated at the appropriate times and
stages of life, taking the responsibility for managing the
Catholic primary schools of the parish, and so on? Or is it
to be a focus point where people are brought into contact
with the person and gospel of Jesus Christ, hear a call to
become disciples and be sent on mission and, in so doing,
be drawn into community with others? Is it to be the place
where the poor are privileged, and neither patronised or
pitied? 'Mission or Maintenance' to borrow the title of a
book published in the seventies?

In other words, does the church exist for itself, or for
bringing God's reign to earth? I think it's fair to say that for
the most part the church in Ireland is seen, and expected to
be, its own *raison d'être*. Those with 'missionary vocations'

have always gone abroad, and the poor at home have not really been heard. The insight of Vatican II that 'the church on earth is by its very nature missionary' (AG 2) didn't seem to apply here in Ireland. After all, Ireland is a Christian country isn't it? But if so, what should we do about 'proclaiming good news to the poor' as a sign of the presence of Jesus among us? Somehow this bit of the gospel seems to have got buried. When Bishop Helder Camara wrestled with its implications, his experience was that 'when I give help to the poor, people call me a saint; when I ask why they are poor, people call me a communist'.

Some years ago I had the idea that I would like to be a missionary 'out foreign' and that I would ask to be transferred to one of our communities in Latin America. I sought advice, and it was suggested that I should live with the idea for a while to see how it would evolve. After some months the desire began to wane, as I began to realise that if I wanted to work with the poor, I should start in my own country, because it is in the industrialised 'North' of the world that the policies are made which largely decide the fate of the poor in the 'South'. Later, having had a job which entailed doing some travel in what we still call the 'Third World', I gained a related insight which has continued to deepen: that our consumer-based capitalist-directed societies are the new territory for evangelisation. The church must be missionary *here in Ireland*.

Why? Because the individualist, consumer values promoted by 'free-market' capitalism – and rampant in Ireland as elsewhere – are the total antithesis of the gospel and bring about the social divisions and exclusion that so mark our world today. Many Irish families, for example, no matter how carefully they budget, cannot stretch their money from week to week, let alone deal with an emergency, such as a late-night doctor's call to a sick child. In fact, the remark, 'if you get sick, don't get sick at a weekend' is common enough in some areas. There is, further, the ongoing tragedy of living as a divided people in one small island and now, sadly, the huge task of rebuilding a process which can establish once again the momentum for a just peace.

The Indian Jesuit, Michael Amaladoss, in a recent article,[1] highlights the structural perspectives that need to nourish our understanding of mission today. 'Charity', in the traditional sense of poverty alleviation, is not enough, he says. It must be complemented by an effort to tackle the underlying causes, and this often demands grappling with the complex global dimensions of the situation. Continued and worsening poverty in Africa, for example, has, as one of its major causes, the economic and trade policies dictated by First World powers for their own advantage. Could we not then say, he continues, that it is more urgent today to preach the good news in the First World? The West has traditionally been regarded as the Christian and mission-sending region of the globe, but this merely serves, now, to heighten the challenge of evangelisation and even, as has been hinted above, to make it more difficult.

In Ireland we have, at the beginning of 1996, a thriving economy, yet 'poverty, unemployment and exclusion will continue to be the core experience of a great many people's lives'.[2] Almost one third of the population lives below the acceptable minimum level of income, and CORI says that there are more people living in poverty today than there were twenty years ago, 'no matter where one draws the poverty line.'[3] This, it is argued, is the result of a failure in successive government policies. But is it just a failure of good intentions? Or do our elected representatives not think it a good political risk to tackle poverty in any comprehensive way? There are few votes in anti-poverty strategies ... So we continue to need voluntary agencies like the St Vincent de Paul Society, *Crosscare, Focus Point* and so on, to plug the gaps which cannot be filled because governments are unable to plan for a greater redistribution of wealth – or will not take the risk of doing so. And while churches in middle class areas still continue to contribute generously to the 'charities', the awkward questions remain unanswered.

It is the same for the 'Third World'. We are enormously generous in contributing to the various agencies calling on us, especially at peak times of 'natural disaster'. But it is much more difficult to get across the message that structural change is required in the political and economic relations which our industrialised countries have with the South. Yet this is exactly what Amaladoss suggests must be part of the church's mission today.

Challenge
There are, of course, cultural challenges in all of this. What kind of values do we want to live by? Values that produce and perpetuate divisiveness at all levels, or the kind which break down barriers? This is where the church could play a leading role. It professes the gospel which points the way to an alternative 'inclusive' society based on love, and gives us the guarantee that the Holy Spirit is with us in working towards this. Yet the church's involvement in society is piecemeal, restricted. But thankfully the prophetic message is being proclaimed and acted out in various ways in Ireland, frequently by agencies or individuals not linked to the church, although some, of course, are. People *are* prepared to come together and put their best energies and talents into what they perceive to be life-enhancing for their neighbourhoods, especially for children and young people.

I recall, some years ago, a young man who was among the first of the families moving into a new housing area where I was living at the time. He was disabled, and in receipt of a disability pension. But his first thought was to organise a summer project for the children, and also to offer himself as a sort of one-man Citizen's Advice Bureau – to put his own knowledge of the 'system' at the service of others who would need to negotiate with the 'Welfare'. (He knew the ropes!)

Where I live now, an area with a population of about 20,000, there are well over sixty different local community-based organisations, all dedicated to the well-being of the people. I think that this brings us close to the heart of the gospel – the call to community – to be enabled to move beyond differences to reconciliation – to gather in mutual love and service. 'That they all may be one, as you, Father, are in me and I in you, that they also may be one in us' (Jn 17:21). The paradox of this call is that it brings with it the division that the gospel also speaks of – between those who hear the call to conversion and those who, like the rich man, turn away. We must not avoid the paradox. So how do we work this out in Ireland where almost one in three of our sisters and brothers lives in poverty, and where the frozen political attitudes of some, both North and South, make reconciliation almost impossible?

Poverty isn't just an economic phenomenon. It means not being able to choose; not having anything to hope for; very rarely having sufficient social skills and self-motivation to look for a way to improve one's situation, or to speak or take initiatives. Even worse, poverty attacks the human spirit, deadening creativity, leaving you feeling vulnerable, worthless, thrown aside. That is the underlying reason why 60-80% of people in many housing estates and inner city areas are unemployed, and why the majority will

never experience what it is like to have something worth-
while to get up in the morning for – unless it is for a short-
term training course or low paid work 'scheme'. The cries
of despair and loneliness are most often silent, but is it any
wonder that they sometimes issue in violence? That young
people turn to drugs or alcohol to deaden the pain?
Recently, in a small area of Dublin's inner city, four young
men died of drug overdoses in the space of about ten days.
Not one of these deaths made it into any of the media.
Were their lives not important too? Yes. But these young
men belonged to a community which is effectively excluded
from taking part in society. Where is our Esther, our
Moses, to give words to the people's cries and bring them
to God and to public hearing? Is there no place where their
voice could have been heard?

The Prophetic Task
Where is the 'heart vision', the spiritual energy that allows
us to see and hear and judge and act in the light of the
Spirit? Spirituality, as we call it, or the lack of it, is, I believe, central to the church's crisis today. A missionary,
heart-responsive spirituality for today would listen to the
cries of the excluded, feel and share the anger, the bleak
despair. And it would give them words. Yes, God listens,
but God listens through the ears of other people too, and
as one who knows only too well the cost of trying to do
this listening and articulating has written: 'nothing could
be more simple, more resisted or more needed. And nothing is more difficult and more painful to sustain in any
place where life is cheap.'

The first prophetic task is, then, to articulate lament, for
the evil must first be recognised and named. In the naming
is the power to overcome it, eventually. The naming is the
prophetic task. An act of faith and of hope. It is also a political task, for politics has to enter into prophecy. Both are

facets of an integral spirituality, and are expressed in worship. 'Do this in remembrance of me' was not just a request to celebrate the Mass on Sunday, but to worship as Jesus did – in the integrity of one's life.

The majority of people in areas like mine don't go to Mass. For many reasons. Some don't even know that that's the church across the road from where they live. Others are too pre-occupied with the daily grind of survival to think of setting time aside for going to church. Some young people, if they think about it at all, don't go because 'it's boring. Always the same old stuff.' For all the effort expended by hard-working pastors, it seems clear that the central task of evangelisation has not been reached: the majority have not been brought into vital contact with Jesus Christ. He is a stranger to them. The church puts the cart before the horse but still expects it to go forward somehow.

What if the churches were to close down and try to begin again by going out to gather small groups of people around matters of local concern which would be linked to the reading of God's word? It would be slow certainly. Some people would go to other parishes for the traditional style of worship. The eyes of others would light up. It would point a way to a more authentic Christian community, as has been discovered in Latin America and other places where it has been tried. It is far too radical a step for us to take all at once, of course – and those who continue to need the 'traditional' must be served as well – but the crisis within the church is at base a structural one, and not one resulting simply from the perceived failure of individuals. So what Jesus said about new wine needing new wineskins applies. It is a question of recognising what is essential, and disentangling ourselves from all non-essential 'trimmings' that centuries of church practice have handed down to us, and becoming free to find where the gospel is leading us now. For me, anyway, as a woman within the institutional church, this is absolutely vital.

We who are the church badly need to listen. But in order to hear we have to switch off other voices – and they are many today – coming from many sources. I believe that our spirituality is weak and inadequate because we have become compromised and taken in, often unknowingly, by the dominant Western ideologies of today. In his book *The Prophetic Imagination*[4] (which, although written from a North American perspective, is extremely relevant and helpful for coming to grips with what is happening here in Ireland today), Walter Brueggemann speaks of the need for 'prophetic ministry'. This prophetic ministry (ideally in our situation, the church) must address, not specific public crises, but 'in season and out of season, the dominant crisis that is enduring and resilient, of having our alternative vocation co-opted and domesticated'.[5] But what do we mean by 'alternative' he asks? Especially if the faith community has become so accustomed to its rituals that it doesn't even understand that there are any alternatives? What he would urge is that prophetic ministry would have as its focus the task of 'evolving, forming and reforming an alternative community'.[6] This means, as I understand it, going beyond talking about what a faith community should be, to searching for and implementing expressions of what we would want it to be. There are many people longing for a chance to do this.

'Without a Vision ...'
How come to such an all-embracing alternative? For this we need both imagination and memory, but we're lacking in both. 'Without a vision, the people perish' (Prov 29:18). The church in Ireland doesn't have a vision out of which its life and energy could flow, since it exists and structures itself more for its own survival. It is like a head without a

heart, and sometimes the head even buries itself in the
ground, ostrich-like. It would be so nice if the clock would
turn backward. There are quite a few people who seriously
see this as the way forward. But with a sense of history, especially of biblical history, we know that crisis periods
have always hit God's people, and yet there were always
those who refused to capitulate to the prevailing mood. In
fact crises became times of purification – *kairos* moments of
grace, of conversion. How badly we need to seize the present moment and allow it to utter its burning cry, and
become a word of God to us, just as it was for Jeremiah:

> The word of Yahweh has meant for me
> insult, derision, all day long.
> I used to say, 'I will not think about him,
> I will not speak in his name any more.'
> Then there seemed to be a fire burning in my heart,
> imprisoned in my bones.
> The effort to restrain it wearied me.
> I could not bear it. (Jer 20:8b-9)

If the church were to reclaim and put its faith once more in
the dynamic power of the gospel, this remembering would
be a source of new vision. We would then 'dare to say' the
Our Father, in full awareness that praying this prayer in-
volves us in a huge risk – an act of faith that God will take
us seriously and involve us more deeply in the struggle to
make God's dream a reality on earth. Worship would then
become a 'high risk invitation', instead of a daily or weekly
ritual that we Christians go to, or even, 'get in'. It would
involve us in the reality of our community's stories, it
would allow us to envision and begin to shape an alternative story, based on the remembered story of Jesus. Then
the poor would become central once again to the church's
concern and ministry, and not just a side-issue. For this to
happen we need, first of all, to humbly confess that we

have allowed the gospel of Jesus to become a stumbling-block to ourselves by the way we have domesticated it. We have not lived according to the standards of the Sermon on the Mount. Yet,

> particularly in our contemporary world of violence and counter-violence, of oppression from the right and the left, of the rich getting richer and the poor poorer, it is imperative for the church-in-mission to include the 'superior justice' of the Sermon on the Mount (Mt 5:20) in its missionary agenda. Its mission cannot concern itself exclusively with the personal, inward, spiritual and 'vertical' aspects of people's lives. Such an approach suggests a dichotomy totally foreign to the Jesus tradition as interpreted by Matthew.[7]

A friend of mine, very involved in her local community, and who describes herself as a Christian socialist, would agree with the above. She feels very angry that the Jesus of the gospel was replaced, in her experience, by a Jesus who inculcated submissiveness and a faith that was portrayed as unconnected to the issues of the day. She is convinced that this was a symptom of a desire to control. She is personally fortunate to be living in a parish where a strong link is made between issues of faith and life, but if she were not, she would have no nourishment for her discipleship. How many more are like her, though less fortunately located!

It has been relatively easy for me to write my dream for what the church might begin to become. I do not have an institutional role. I have full freedom to dream. Nevertheless I do not believe that this absolves me of all responsibility to play my part with others in the community who may also dream. And this I am fortunate enough to be able to do. As a result I have some small insight into the pressures that clergy responsible for maintaining parishes are under, and the expectations attached to their role, and I have great admiration for the ways in which they struggle to respond.

In speaking of the church in Ireland and what I perceive to be its weaknesses, I don't separate myself from it. I am part of it all, and, as a religious, part of a body struggling with the same issues of how to live an authentic faith in a highly divided consumer society. I have a concern that much of the spiritual nourishment on offer today for Christians in Ireland encourages a certain spiritual consumerism. I see little help for those trying to bridge the gap between what goes on around them and their faith, though there are hon-ourable exceptions. I am not denying that Christians need time apart. According as life speeds up and the pressures pile on, taking time to be silent, to reflect, to unwind, to get in touch with God's word and with oneself, become more urgent if we hope to have anything to offer to others. Perhaps parishes could provide more opportunities for people to do this – half-days or evenings or, for those with a little more time, weekends away. Relationships need spec-ial time for deeper knowing. A relationship with God is no exception, and many thirst for a way into this.

Which Way?
We are at a crossroads in Ireland. A number of directions present themselves, some of which I have mentioned. I think of Robert Frost's poem *The Road Not Taken*, and won-der if we, as church, will have the courage to make a choice. The point is to know where we are starting from, and then to choose a direction. Frost would have preferred not to have to choose, and both roads seemed equally at-tractive, yet he took the plunge and went ahead. The poem's ending is ambiguous, and doesn't say clearly that it turned out to be the best choice. Choosing is risky, and

whatever path we take we won't see the promised land. In
fact we will only be starting the journey.

A biblical image for this would be the Exodus. Is this where
the Irish church should begin? Pilgrims setting out on a
journey need to take certain things with them, while ensuring that they travel lightly. One of the most important
of these travelling-bag contents must be hope. And hope is
something that I believe we Christians greatly need to
nourish, so that we can offer something different to the
prevailing cynicism, burn-out and despair prevalent within
as well as outside the church. I do not speak of optimism,
for which there are few obvious grounds. Hope is a far
tougher article. But to choose hope is a risk.

Again we come back to the need to listen. The institutional
church will have to rediscover how to do this; it has spent
so much time speaking. Hopes are being expressed as well
as grief and anger, and these come from many sources –
from solidarity groups to pop singers to poets as well as
from some preachers. The church will be all the richer if it
can recognise and seize this present moment. There are so
many beautiful passages from Isaiah to encourage this
stance, and I will end with this one:

> Thus says Yahweh ...
> No need to recall the past,
> no need to think about what was done before.
> See, I am doing a new deed,
> even now it comes to light: can you not see it?
> Yes, I am making a road in the wilderness,
> paths in the wilds ...
> I am putting water in the wilderness ...
> to give my chosen people drink.
> The people I have formed for myself
> will sing my praises. (Is 43:16, 18-19, 20b-21)

Notes:

1. 'New Faces of Mission', *Indian Missiological Review*, September 1995.
2. Budget Response 1996, CORI Justice Office.
3. Ibid.
4. *The Prophetic Imagination*, Walter Brueggemann, Fortress Press, 1978.
5. Ibid, p 13.
6. Ibid, p 14.
7. *Transforming Mission, Paradigm Shifts in Theology of Mission*, David J. Bosch, Orbis Books, Maryknoll, New York, 1993.

Are we busy about the right things?

Séamus Ryan

Three stories: here is the first:
It was around the mid-sixties, about thirty years ago. Two
young people from a provincial town getting married.
We'll call them Ruth and Michael. No church wedding for
them. Registry Office in Dublin, and a bit of a celebration
with their families and friends afterwards. Their decision
would hardly be news in these times, but it was novel then
and created a stir in the local community. I was friendly
with one of the families and the parents approached me,
anxious to give some religious dimension to their daughter's wedding. A kind of compromise was reached whereby
the couple agreed, rather reluctantly, to attend Mass after
their wedding in the quiet chapel of a neighbouring con-
vent. When we arrived in Molesworth Street on that fine
summer morning, Michael said it would mean a great deal
to both of them if I would come along to the Registry
Office. My heart said I should go, but my head was telling
me that in the eyes of my church this was no marriage and
that the presence of the priest would be misconstrued, so I
stayed in my car while everybody else went with the couple. How it would be improper for me to be there, but OK
to celebrate the eucharist with them afterwards does not
seem to have occurred to me. The couple came to the Mass
out of deference to their parents, but they took little part.
After all, I had declined to take any part in what was important to them.

Another story. This time far from home, and twenty-five
years later. I was on sabbatical, spending six months in

India. There had been a fair measure of exposure to Hinduism, but I was eager to get some lived experience of Buddhism. I was advised to sign up for a ten-day meditation course at an International Buddhist Centre in Igatpuri, about two hundred miles north of Bombay. It was truly being thrown in at the deep end! Ten hours of meditation per day for ten days. The goal was liberation and enlightenment: learning the art of living through being enabled by meditation to see things as they really are. There was an obvious affinity with some Judaeo-Christian themes: a yearning for wisdom, deliverance from evil (in thought and in deed), the need for quiet and space in one's life, the gift of new sight. But in other respects the two faiths seemed poles apart: the serene Siddhattha Gotama living peacefully into extreme old age; Jesus of Nazareth dying a terrible death on a Roman gibbet. Which of them speaks to us more profoundly of the mystery of life and God?

Some people from Europe were undergoing this Buddhist experience for the third or fourth time, and were over the moon about it. I had the good fortune on the day we were leaving (no communication was permitted between the participants during the ten days) to share a few hours with a Hindu Sanyassi, one of those remarkable sages who spend their time tramping around India, his whole possessions in a travelling bag slung on his shoulder. He made an extraordinary impression on me, a rare individual, so carefree, so assured in his own Hindu faith, yet so prepared to learn what was good in another's. I will never forget his parting words: 'Of course you have something to learn from us here in India, but your task is to listen to the God who addresses you in Jesus, and to respond to him with all your heart. It is there you will find the light and life you need.' Wise and thoughtful words. They still challenge me. I will return to them.

A third and final anecdote. Recently I was recovering from a hip operation in a Dublin hospital. I became quite friendly with one of the women who came to clean my room during the fortnight I was there. Here is her story. A mother of seven children, and after twenty years together her husband just walked out on her. She was able to retain the house but needed the cleaning job in order to have sufficient money to take care of the children. After the separation she went through an agonising time, feeling a deep sense of rejection and drifting from one form of depression to another. She continued to attend Sunday Mass, but seemed to get nothing from it. A friend introduced her to a small group of Christians who met with a leader once a week to listen to a passage from the bible, to share memories or stories evoked by the passage, to pray together, and to share a cup of tea. She has now left her own local Catholic church and become a regular member of this group. She found community and support there at a time of great loneliness. If she missed a meeting someone would ring up or call around to see if she were well. A vague sense of guilt brought her back to Mass in her local parish church one Sunday morning, but nobody even noticed that she had been away. She had not been missed. She has never returned.

In the more intimate group she became aware for the first time that she was precious to God, and that she was loved just as she is. She learned a new appreciation of the bible, and a love of God's word. She was encouraged to share her own thoughts on a passage of scripture, and people listened. On one occasion the group organised a weekend away together, where she was encouraged to recognise and acknowledge her own unique gifts. The experience gave her a whole new sense of herself and of her personal worth. In fact a whole new life had begun for her since becoming a part of this small group. In her local church she had been just another anonymous parishioner, lost in the crowd. She felt angry now that over all those years nobody had opened up the treasure of the scriptures for her, or helped her to pray with the word of God. Another story worth pondering.

People of the Kingdom

All three stories give me a starting point for some reflections about church and parish and ministry in Ireland today. It may be best to begin with the Indian experience. Even five years later, the deep religious experience of those ten days is still with me; the earnest quest of those hundreds of people (the vast majority of them students and young single men) for wisdom and enlightenment in their lives; the altogether unforgettable peace and serenity of the Hindu Sanyassi, and his gentle words of counsel to seek God in Jesus of the gospels. The whole experience brought home to me how important is the insight of the Second Vatican Council, that the church is not to be thought of primarily as an organised hierarchy with Pope, bishops and priests as its most vital elements. The church is essentially a *people*, where everybody has some kind of mission, according to their gifts. Even people who do not believe in Christ, but have faith in God, belong there. Also those who do not believe in God, but yet have some awareness of life's depth and mystery, participate in a real way in the life of this people of God. The same Council reminds us that the Holy Spirit offers to all men and women the opportunity of being partners in God's grand design, in ways often known only to God alone.[1] Thus, we find the Lord reassuring an anxious Paul in Corinth: 'Do not be afraid, but speak...I am with you … for I have many people in this city.'[2] St Augustine is well known for his broad open-ended concept of church, somehow enfolding and embracing all humanity. The boundary lines are not so sharply drawn between those who belong to God's people and those who seem excluded. We do well to listen to his words: 'There are many whom God has, and the church does not have them. And there are many whom the church has, and God does not have them at all.'

My Sanyassi friend reminds me of those people we have the good fortune to meet who have a radiant goodness about them, even though they seem to have no contact with any church. Jesus himself discovered a quality of faith in the Roman centurion that he had not found amongst his own people, and that 'pagan's' prayer is found on our lips every Sunday at one of the most solemn moments of the eucharist. There is a greater reality than can be fully captured in any church or religion. Jesus called it God's kingdom, God's reign, and his whole mission was dedicated to it.

At the heart of the kingdom is a new way of understanding God. Between the Adonai of Sinai and the Abba of the gospel there lies a long journey. Jesus experiences God as Abba, as Father, in a most tender, intimate way. He is sustained throughout his life by the unshakeable conviction of being always held in his Father's loving care: 'I am not alone because the Father is with me.'[3] In the great solemn prayer before his passion, Jesus says unequivocally that the same Father's love reaches out to embrace all those now bonded with Jesus. It must be one of the most incredible words of the gospel. Because he is word made flesh, and now mysteriously one with every man and woman, everyone – even the very least of his brethren, even you or I – is held in the same unconditional love by this prodigal Father.[4]

Jesus befriended people and spent time with them ('Master, where do you live?' 'Come and see.') in order to bring them to the same Abba-awareness, the same convict-

ion of the Father's all-embracing love which was the driving
force of his own life. Of course, Jesus did more than talk
about the Father's love. He was the living example of it in
all he said and did. And so the apostle could say: 'We have
heard it, we have seen it with our own eyes. We have
watched, and touched it with our own hands; the word of
life ... a life made visible to us.'[5]

It seems clear from the gospels that Jesus fulfilled his mission simply through being with people. Men and women
look to the church and its ministers today for an echo of
the Jesus of Nazareth who proclaimed the presence of the
reign of God, through the quality of his own presence with
people, and particularly through his reaching out to the
poor and the outcast. 'God was with him,' says Peter, 'and
he went about doing good, and caring for all who had fall-
en under the power of the devil. And we are witnesses to
everything he did throughout the countryside of Judea
and in Jerusalem itself.'[6]

He was a man of his time and he knew his people: the
farmers of the land, the fishermen of the lake, the money-
changers of the city. Nothing seemed to escape him: the
blind beggar restrained by the crowd; the children kept
out of sight by the disciples; the woman touching the hem
of his garment; the little operator Zacchaeus high on his
tree; the widow putting her few pence in the Temple box.
The priest today, the Council has told us, is called to make
Jesus present. This is not meant to separate him from the
everyday world he shares with other men and women. If
he is, in some sense, a man apart, it can only be in the way
Jesus was. 'Priests cannot be of service to men,' the same
Vatican II reminds us, 'if they remain strangers to the life
and conditions of men.'[7]

Fellow-travellers?

But strangers we too often are. Those years in the seminary sow the seeds of later segregation. The relative seclusion of the presbytery may well repel rather than attract both the seeker and the stranger. Celibacy and clerical dress contribute further to the sense of 'separateness'. It seems to me now, looking back over the training we received, that priests of my vintage were better equipped for the ministry of 'doing things' for people, rather than for the pilgrim task of simply being with them on a common journey. The quiet years in Nazareth were doubtless a necessary prelude to the public ministry of Jesus. We were better at the 'doing' than the 'being': saying Mass, hearing confessions, baptising the infants, anointing the infirm, blessing all manner of objects, making the public speech. But we were not proficient, I think, in the more demanding skills required in being a fellow pilgrim, particularly over rough terrain. It has been suggested that we were more at home in the role of the mechanic than of the gardener, geared for efficient performance, rather than the nurturing of life and growth.[8]

'We are companions on life's journey': the words of a popular hymn. That's it; that's what I should be, a companion to people, and allow them to companion me. In the end of the day what is the greatest gift anyone has to offer? Not some little learning or some little skill, useful though they may be, but the gift of myself. Jesus did not just *inaugurate* the kingdom; he *was himself* the kingdom. We are the earthenware vessels that carry this treasure, much more through what we are than in what we do. We are the Body of Christ, we are the word made flesh for others. In their faith, ordinary people often have access to a theology and a spirituality which others learn only at second-hand from books. The parish priest was visiting the old lady who lived alone on his round of visits. He was laying out the book and the oils when she said to him: 'Father, sit down for a while first, and we'll have a smoke and a chat.' Christ present in the minister, a real presence, Paul VI assures us. The presence of another that is truly real is the most healing thing in the world.

One of the emphases of Vatican II is on the church as communion. It is a communion rooted ultimately in the mystery of the triune God.[9] This has important implications for all church ministry, and especially for the priest. If his primary task is not 'to run the parish' but to enable communion to grow, then the quality of his relationships with his people will be central to his ministry. The quality of personal care and friendship between the members of a parish team, or a parish council or core-group, will be as important as the tasks they are engaged in.[10]

It is not uncommon to hear that priests are very busy. I believe it. But are we busy about the right things? Perhaps more than anything else we need to read and re-read the gospels. There is no denying how central to the mission of Jesus was the ministry of healing. Few would deny that we live in a world where there are very many broken people. How does the church, the parish, continue the Lord's ministry of healing today? My experience with the woman in the hospital is increasingly the story of many who come to the church seeking help and healing, but find they have to look elsewhere. We need to listen again to the disconcerting parable about the evil tenants (Mt 21). Jesus was accosting the Jewish religious leaders of his time, but the parable is equally disturbing for ourselves today if we fail to bear witness effectively to Jesus Christ and the gospel of the kingdom. Of us, too, it might be said: 'The kingdom of God will be taken away from you, and given to a people bearing the fruits of it.'

Small is beautiful

We hear a good deal today from various sources about the drift of people from the Catholic church to Evangelical churches in the United States and Latin America. The phenomenon is not unknown here, especially in more disadvantaged areas. What is drawing them away? Research in the US suggests acceptance and relatedness as major factors.[11] The Vatican report, *Sects, Cults, and New Religious Movements*, acknowledges that some Catholics leave their parishes because of coldness and animosity. Obviously there is no single cause. Here are two of the factors most commonly cited which seem to attract people to other churches:

1. A wider range of services to help meet individual needs. A greater flexibility within a structured worship which serves to encourage more participation. People speak about the help they receive through hearing other people share their experience of God. They are encouraged to discern where God may be a power in their own lives.

2. A more profound experience of community through membership of smaller groups. We saw a good example of this in the case of my hospital friend. The American theologian, Dick Westley, explores the paradox that real community is built not around our talents and achievements, but rather on our shared weakness and frailty. Too often, while our strengths divide us, our weakness disarms us and enables us to be one. Small groups of ordinary Christians, meeting in the familiar surrounds of their own homes, help to create an ambience where people seem more prepared to let go of their need to appear self-sufficient, and share with each other their common human frailty. It is only in the acknowledgment of shared weakness that the real strength of community is born.[12] If we might take some liberty with the words of St Paul: 'For the sake of Christ, then, we are content with weaknesses ... for when we are weak, then we are strong'(2 Cor 12:10).

The 'signs of the times' seem to be encouraging the formation within parishes of small Christian communities. (Our
word *parish* comes from two Greek words, *par* and *oikos*,
and means, literally, 'beyond the house', suggesting that
the first parishes arose out of families or people gathering
in small groups to pray.) Today, where they are well established, these small Christian communities have four main
ingredients: a) shared prayer, b) shared scripture, c) shared
life stories, d) ministry, within the group, to the parish and
to the world.[13]

Every beginning is small, and one must start, as ever,
where the people are. There is no need to look too far for
groups since all parishes already have people who come
together, bonded by common interest or shared ministry
of some kind. In our own urban parish there is a strong
tradition of little groups of people gathering together in
each other's houses to say the rosary. A beginning can be
made by inviting them to add a reading of scripture and
some shared prayer and reflection to their meetings.
Seasons like Advent and Lent are a good time to introduce
this. We are fortunate to have a parish sister with a good
gift for the formation and encouragement of such house-
groups. She was responsible for more than twenty groups
meeting during Lent, and some of them will continue
through the year. Groups of this kind will go through
stages, just as ordinary relationships do, and will need
careful guidance from an understanding leader. As in all
areas of the church's ministry, leaders will need training
and back-up resources.

When Jesus sent out the seventy-two disciples he sent them
two by two. It would seem that we cannot adequately witness to the good news on our own. 'If two of you on earth
agree to ask anything at all in my name, it will be given to
you by my Father in heaven.' Even the ministry of prayer

is more effective when shared. In a culture of growing individualism, we are rediscovering this vital dimension of the Christian life in all sorts of areas.

'I am the good shepherd. I know my own and my own know me.' The words suggest a style of leadership where there is a mutual knowing and being known, caring and being cared for. In the words of Henri Nouwen, we are wounded healers, fragile and sinful, needing just as much care as those we care for. Recent events in the Irish church have borne out this truth. A style of ministry which does not allow for a mutual 'being ministered to' can all too easily become a subtle way of exercising power over others. It was about this very danger that Jesus sternly warned his church: 'This must not happen among you!' We need to be imaginative in exploring how authority can be used in more creative ways for the re-building of the kingdom.

Trying to be human
I come back to the story with which I began: the small town couple getting married in a registry office in Dublin. I am appalled today at my insensitivity in imposing on them on their wedding day a religious service which they clearly did not want. Thank God we do grow a little wiser with the years. I spoke earlier about the importance of supporting and encouraging signs of the kingdom wherever we find them. Here was this young couple, enthusiastic about pledging their love forever in a civil marriage in the presence of their friends. And they really wanted me to be there! Had I listened to my heart and been more concerned for the kingdom and its values, it is there I should have been. Wasn't Jesus himself a great one for going to weddings, and ensuring the wine would flow and the best of it? But I listened to the church, or what I thought to be the church's wisdom, and proved myself to be most of all lacking in humanity and love.

Teilhard de Chardin has this to say:

> The greatest objection brought against Christianity
> in our time, and the real source of the distrust which
> insulates entire blocks of humanity from the influ-
> ence of the church, has nothing to do with historical
> or theological difficulties. It is the suspicion that our
> religion makes its followers inhuman.

Teilhard has always been a hero of mine, and he touches a
deep chord with me here. Among men especially, I find an
embarrassment about religion, a reluctance towards any
depth of commitment which, I suspect, is not simply to be
explained by shyness or mere indifference. There may be
uneasiness about a church which is too much 'church' and
not enough Christian community, embarrassment about
getting involved with a whole dimension of life which is
foreign to them and might suggest to their friends a dimin-
ishment of their humanity. Strange, isn't it, in a church
whose founder attracted those rugged fishermen of
Galilee around him, and who came 'that men may have
life and have it to the full'? Vatican II was concerned with
redressing an imbalance when it stressed the essential
humanness of all true holiness in one of its great seminal
statements:

> Whoever follows after Christ, the perfect man,
> becomes himself more of a man. (*Gaudium et Spes*, 41)

Another Frenchman, and one of the great men of the
Council, Yves Congar, responds well to Teilhard (he is
speaking of priests):

> We must in some way be devoted to both parties be-
> tween whom we are mediators; devoted wholly on
> high to the things of faith, devoted wholly below to
> all the hurly-burly of human activity. We have to be
> men of God, but also men of men.

Another spiritual giant of our times, who struggled to keep the balance articulated so well by Congar, was Thomas Merton. In her biography, Monica Furlong says of him:

> As the years stripped away the obvious answers ... he felt himself to be left with little but his humanity ... He began to see that the highest spiritual development was to be ordinary, to be fully a human being in the way few human beings succeed in becoming, so simple and naturally themselves.

We are here on earth to become human beings. The sentiment of Vatican II cited above could be a possible focus around which to organise the agenda of a parish. It would be difficult to surpass it as a mission statement.

I said earlier that the priest or pastoral worker needs to be more of the gardener, less of the mechanic. There is a further image from the gardening world which speaks with some power to my own life and my experience of priesthood over the latter third of this century. Even those with little gardening experience will be familiar with the pot-bound plant. The plant begins to wilt and wither. It has been in the container too long; the roots have nowhere to go, simply round and round inside the pot, eventually strangling and choking the plant. The roots are yearning to break out, to find more space, more soil, a new ambience in which to flourish and grow. After thirty-five years I have a sense of a priesthood that is pot-bound: too encased with a narrow clerical concept of authority, too fearful to break out of the confinement imposed by the expectations of people who yearn for 'the security of familiar ground' and who would keep us pot-bound in a style of ministry that is evidently no longer as effective or attractive as it might be.

Death into Life

But there is always hope. Where there are signs of death, there are also signs of life. Left to ourselves, as a church or as individuals, there is an innate tendency to cling to what we have grown accustomed to, long after it has outlived its usefulness. But the God of the bible is a God of Exodus, a resourceful God to get us moving again. The early Desert Fathers believed that sometimes God has first to bind us in order to set us free. In a great Advent prayer, we call on this turbulent God to 'break open the heavens' and come to save us. On the longest night of the year, we call on the Key of David to 'bring us out of the dungeon where we are sitting bound in the darkness and in the shadow of death'.

We have been doing it 'our way' for too long, and it is only through some kind of death and resurrection that we can be led to find 'God's way' again. The poet often says it better than the theologian:

> Batter my heart, three-personned God, for you
> as yet but knock, breathe, shine and seek to mend;
> that I may rise and stand, o'erthrow me, and bend
> your force to break, blow, burn and make me new.
> — John Donne, *Sonnets*

Notes:
1. *Lumen Gentium* 15, 16; *Gaudium et Spes* 22.
2. Acts 18:9.
3. John 16:32.
4. *Lumen Gentium* 22.
5. 1 John 1.
6. Acts 10:39.
7. *Decree on Priests* 3.
8. Nicholas Harnan, *The Heart's Journey Home*, Indiana, 1992.

9. *Lumen Gentium* 22.

10. Cf. *The Sign We Give, Report of the Working Party on Collaborative Ministry*, Bishops' Conference of England and Wales, 1995.

11. Cf. W. Bausch, *The Total Parish Manual,* p 25, Columba Press 1994.

12. Dick Westley, *Good Things Happen*, pp 36-7, XXIIIrd Publications 1994.

13. Cf. Patrick Brennan, *Parishes that Excel*, p 10, Crossroad 1993.

14. Cf. My article in *The Furrow*, April 1996.

A Response:
The Disengaged

John Dunlop

Anne Looney's story of young people with blank faces who failed to make any experiential connection with Lent is powerful in its description of us 'being a changing people living in a changing place'. I wonder if the rate of change is more pronounced in the Republic than in Northern Ireland and, if so, is it because it has been such a predictably homogenous Catholic place for so long and until so recently? What a comparative outsider like myself finds so interesting is that what appeared to be such a self-confident institution should so quickly have found itself in a crisis.

I wrote that Anne Looney's story is a description of 'us' for, while I am a Presbyterian living in Northern Ireland, the cultural and ideological forces operating so powerfully for change in the Republic of Ireland are operating here as well, but from a different starting point, since this has never been such a homogenous place. While the violence of the last twenty-five years has kept us in a predictable and familiar mindset of unresolved constitutional issues, change has been happening at another level.

Many Protestants in Northern Ireland have been conditioned to thinking that the threat to the existence of Protestant churches, and the associated Protestant community, came from the intolerant ultramontanism of a universally confident Roman Catholicism. The real threat which we now face is not from that source at all but from the increasingly per-

vasive secularisation of people's thinking, which makes
thought or talk of God the equivalent of contemplating
something over the horizon, out of sight and out of mind.
For an increasing number of people, faith lives at best out
of memory rather than contemporary engagement.

Many, mainly young people, have ceased to practise the
faith in terms of regular attendance at worship. While that
is true of many, it is not true of all. Increasingly, those who
do worship regularly do so, not out of custom or primary
commitment to the church, but out of faith in God, which
faith is expressed in commitment and involvement in what
we and they are about as part of a community of believers.

There is a danger in Ireland that we talk about the church
rather than about God. It has been said that people in this
country, maybe particularly in the Republic, will talk end-
lessly about the church and its influences and problems
and its bishops and priests, but when the conversation
turns to God things get very sticky indeed. Maybe such
talk about the church is better than indifference. But, if
people get the church confused with God, then the inevitable frailty of the church will lead to the abandonment
of faith in God. Dietrich Bonhoeffer wrote, in *Life Together*,
that the sooner we get disillusioned with the church the
better, for we will then learn that the church lives by the
grace of God. He went on to say that the sooner we subse-
quently get disillusioned with ourselves the better, for we
will understand that we too live by the grace of God. The
primary reality is not the church but the grace of God, and
all else, including worship and service, is response to the
generosity of God's grace.

Community
At the heart of the church resides the grace of God, ener-
gised by the Holy Spirit and witnessed to by symbols and

signs. Grace is the open-hearted compassion of a loving, relational God who dwells in the unity and community of the Trinity, and who invites us into fellowship and engagement. It seems to me that relational concepts and relational experiences are crucially important.

John R. W. Stott described modern urban society as being characterised by 'proximity without community'. Proximity without community also describes what happens to people in many churches. They enter from loneliness and leave as isolated as they came in.

How can people experience a sense of belonging in a large church? Most Presbyterian churches were designed with narrow aisles and small vestibules. When the service finishes, conversation causes traffic jams as other worshippers squeeze past those who wish to talk. Thoughtfulness for the interests of those who wish to leave quickly leads to the absence of conversation and, before people know where they are, they are out in the rain and physically and metaphorically out in the cold. This has led some congregations to remove a number of pews from the back of their churches to create meeting areas, where coffee is sometimes served and communication is facilitated. Some recently-designed buildings have large vestibules where conversation before and after the service becomes possible.

An experience of community is mediated in many Presbyterian churches through the pastoral work of ministers who visit homes regularly and build up good personal relationships with members of the congregation. While people in a large church may not know one another, at least they know the minister, who also knows them. The down side of this is that it does not enable people to escape from a form of clerical dependency into widespread interpersonal Christian community. In some churches, small fel-

lowship and bible study groups are an essential part of the
overall life of the congregation, but they generally only involve a small percentage of the whole. Interpersonal fellowship is also facilitated during the week in the multi-
tude of small organisations, both for young people and
adults, which constitute the week-long activities of the average congregation.

Since only a minority of people are going to attend small
groups for fellowship and Christian education, does adult
Christian education not need to take place in the Sunday
worship services, when word and sacrament are taken
equally seriously? But can we, who are preachers, preach?
A carelessly delivered sermon will do the worshipper no
more good than routinely and thoughtlessly received
bread and wine. Christian worship is a joyous and serious
business which requires faith-filled receptive imagination
on the part of the worshippers, as well as of those who
conduct the services.

Prophets, Priests, Ministers and Leaders
The preceding papers contain urgent calls for prophetic
utterance from the church.

Who is the church? Certainly not only the priests, the ministers, the bishops and the leaders in the diocesan structures and their Protestant equivalents. Catholicism strikes
me as being an interesting ecclesial system, in that there is
room for religious orders represented by organisations
like CORI. But is the voice of CORI not also to be reckoned
with as part of the voice of the church?

There has been a lot of creative work done in the name of
Christ, and in obedience to Christ, and not in the name of
the church. Evangelical parachurch missionary organisations (as well as reconciliation organisations like Corry-

meela) are numerous, are not controlled by any church, but are run by people who worship in churches every Sunday. These organisations are signs of the kingdom and means by which the reign of God is realised. In the widespread world of Protestant evangelicalism, these organisations exist without benefit of clergy in their leadership. Being outside the organisational control of churches, they have more freedom to be innovative.

Recently I have had opportunity to do some work with the Community of St Egidio, which is based in the church of St Egidio in Rome. The church was previously that of an enclosed Carmelite order. It is primarily a lay community, led by lay people in everyday employment. It is recognised by the Vatican. This is a community, without fulltime paid leadership, which lives an alternative life focused on the service of the poor and the making of peace. The life of the community is sustained by regular daily worship and the communal and individual study of the word of God. I see the community as a kind of leaven which challenges and inspires. Leaven exists, not for itself but for the whole, and needs to be leaven to work. This community is part of the church and is therefore a sign of the kingdom to the wider church and to the world.

The worship of the community, as well as its life of service, is singularly marked by imagination, and engages and inspires many young adults who had previously ceased to attend worship in their parish churches. Indeed many had lapsed from the church. They are now deeply involved, having been introduced to the life of the community by their enthusiastically committed peer-group colleagues.

Anne Looney understandably regrets that the 'new voices' on the *Late Late Show* were lost in 'the booming tones of offical churchdom'. Let me suggest that prophetic voices are usually the voices of individuals, or of groups like

CORI, which are free to be prophetic because they do not carry the responsibility of the magisterium of having always to be seen to be right about everything.

An additional problem may be that the voice of 'churchdom' represents the voice of consensus or the perceived safer voice of a known position. By the time the discussion gets through to consensus, the prophetic edge will have been removed. The Vatican Council was perhaps most remarkable in its ability to stay with a sharp edge.

In most situations, the church as 'churchdom' will not be prophetic, but hopefully the same church will produce a few prophets. Some may be bishops and Presbyterian Moderators and Methodist Presidents, but if they are to fill that role they need to be given the freedom not always to be right and not always to conform to the consensus. Through the activity of such dissenters in high places, it may then become clear that there is at best consensus and *not unanimity* in the leadership and, where there is an obvious absence of unanimity, there is freedom; or, to put it another way, diversity exists out in the open.

While the institution may contain both prophets and priests, it may be more difficult for the one individual to be consistently both prophet and priest. The institution may contain both, honour both, give space to both, but perhaps not in the same person. The prophets who become the institutional leaders may suddenly find themselves carrying responsibility for the institution and, in that position, may become cautious and constrained. Maybe the lesson is that a prophet should never become a bishop, unless such a person is a very remarkable individual.

Nevertheless, great benefit accrues from designated leaders being prophets, for room is then created for other people at other levels who are given space to escape from the 'pot-bound' restrictions so clearly described by Séamus Ryan.

Those who know
Anne Looney writes that 'the voice of CORI is heard, for it listens to the new Ireland; it begins in economic and social realities and critiques them with gospel principles and the shared social teaching of the church'.

The prophets have to dialogue with all the strata of the new Ireland, for the upwardly-mobile professionally ambitious are also impoverished without God. In the time of Jesus, as of now, 'a man's life consisteth not in the abundance of the things that he possesseth'; likewise for women.

Carol Dorgan is passionate about the poor and the deprived. She wrote that 'the first prophetic task is to articulate the lament. The evil must first be recognised and named'. My experience is that only those who *know* can do this; and only those who live there can know. Since she knows, she is the prophet. Those of us who have either never lived with the poor or have ceased to do so, never or no longer *know* and cannot articulate the lament about the 'bleak despair' and the daily grind. It's beyond the horizons of our daily experience. The prophetic voice comes from those who live in the wilderness places of urban deprivation.

The oppotunity for experimentation with the Irish equivalent of Basic Ecclesial Communities is there. The numerous community groups in deprived areas indicate that there is no absence of indigenous people with gifts of leadership. What is important is that Christian witness is not collapsed without remainder into social work which has no explicit God dimension, otherwise the poor will only meet the concerned church and never get beyond people to meet God. Should that happen, when those concerned church people retire or die, there will be no one left to witness to the gospel. Meantime the poor will have continued in a dependency relationship with the professionals in the church, and will not have been liberated into the privileges and responsibilities of the priesthood of all believers.

Afterword

Dr John Dunlop's response to the four main essays in this *Exploration* provides a valuable ecumenical dimension to the whole, both in proposing a fresh perspective on the matters discussed and especially in its very vivid illustration of the many-sided relationship between faith, religious tradition and culture. Some of the questions he raises will be familiar to us all, others will be new, either in form or substance or both. And in opening our eyes and minds to a different way of confronting the challenge of the times, he also may provoke us into taking a second look at our own way of doing things.

What he has to say about prophecy in the church may disturb some of us. Let us hope it will.